BIG SIS TALKS

THE CRIMSON KISS QUOTE COLLECTION III

Cici.B

Cici. B
THE CRIMSON KISS

Dedicated to all of the women who have been big sisters to me along the way…

"If you don't know something,
let those who do know educate you,
then share what you've learned
with someone else.
If you've learned something on your own,
still share it with someone else.
Life is about paying it forward, B.
Never forget that."

I didn't forget.

I don't have any biological older sisters, but growing up in my neighbourhood there would always be girls around who were a couple of years older than my group of friends and I, who stayed dropping some serious gems on us. Sometimes it would be when we were fucking up—one of them would pull us aside and give us a good talk explaining why we needed to get our acts together. Sometimes it would be when *they* had fucked up—they would tell us all about it, including the consequences of their fuck ups and why we should avoid doing what they did at all costs. No matter what though, ***they always kept it real with us.*** No filters, no beating around the bush, no "taking it easy" on us, and definitely no coddling, ever.

Their Big Sis Talks were direct, the tone in their voices were dead ass serious and the truths they delivered were often so brutal that they cut deep into our young ass souls and made us cry; but we respected them nonetheless, because we knew they were simply lookin' out for us.

Some of us were hard-headed as fuck and didn't always pick up all of the gems they dropped on the spot, but… let me assure you that the ones we left on the floor definitely came back to bite us in the ass at some point or another in life.

As time went on and I grew through my teens and well into my adulthood, I realized that I'd had *so many women* step in and take on the role of my big sister throughout my life. From friends, to aunts, to women on the internet who don't even know I exist but drop those straight, no chaser gems every day for *all women to hear*, to random women who have seen me crying in my car in a parking lot and took time out of their day to stop, ask me if I was okay, give me some words of encouragement then stay with me until I was good to drive again, right up to my own mother who has always had this ability to step out of mom mode, and into best friend or big sister mode whenever she feels like that's who I need at the moment.

All of these women along the way have given me words, sentences, paragraphs and mottos that have ended up serving me through different versions of myself, and as I continue to do my work (sharing my stories via writing books, social media, etc…) and listening to other women, I realize how important the big sister role truly is, which is exactly what inspired me to put this book together.

Some of the talks you're going to read throughout these pages date as far back as years ago, while others are as recent as a month ago.
Some are talks that have been given *to me* by other women, some are talks that have been given *by me* to other women, and some are talks that I've had to give to my damn self.

Like all of my books, there will be no sugar-coating, and my hope is that when you're finished reading this you:

1- *Feel comforted* in knowing that you're not alone in many of the thoughts you think and feelings you feel.

2- *Come to a realization* about yourself (or many) and confront it/them head on.

3- *Feel empowered and inspired* to get your shit together—whatever corner of you life that you've got some shit in, no matter how big or small the pile—*that* shit.

We all need other women to tell us what we need to hear sometimes, not just what we want to hear because, ***part of women empowerment is telling each other the truth, even when that truth hurts.***

So, here we go…

BIG SIS TALKS

My superpower
is finding a way to overcome
any and every obstacle
that is thrown in my path.
Perhaps, that is your superpower too.

Speak life into yourself

When our homegirls come to us with their hearts filled with pain, crying and explaining how badly they're being treated in their relationships—what do we do?

We get real with them, and we speak life into them.

We remind them of all their amazing qualities, how beautiful they are inside and out, just how much they have to offer, that they don't deserve the shit that is being thrown at them and that what they allow will ultimately continue.

All these same reminders we give to our homegirls when they are with men who don't deserve them…

We've got to learn to start giving to ourselves, too.

Hit that glow-up, Boo

"Make amends with the old versions of yourself; you know, the ones who accepted the bullshit, stayed around for the bullshit and made excuses for the bullshit? Them. Make amends with the old versions of yourself by doing better with the new version of yourself. Hit that glow up, boo."

— *Me to myself... in my mirror.*

Cancel that check, sis

Being a positive person doesn't mean that
you don't ever have bad days.
It doesn't mean you always have a smile
plastered across your face.
It doesn't mean you never feel discouraged.
It doesn't mean you never feel down.

Being a positive person doesn't mean that
negative experiences never affect you…
all it means is that you don't allow yourself
to move in, unpack, and start paying rent to
live in them.

Hey, you, with the good heart...

"It is not your responsibility to fix people though," my aunt said as we sat on her front porch.
"I think deep down I know that," I told her, "but it's almost as if I just can't help myself."
She shook her head, "Well, then you need to *start* helping yourself, because if you don't, you're only going to set yourself up for a lifetime of disappointments. You can be there for people in the best way that you can, so long as it's not fucking up your own mental and emotional health. You can offer them encouragement and a positive environment to which they can gain inspiration from—but *fix* them? No. That is their responsibility, not yours."

It would only be years later, once I was in the process of doing my inner work and began slowly identifying my own problems, that I would get what my aunt told me through my thick ass head (especially when I took what she had said and applied it to one of my most extreme problem areas… men.)

I was broken, and because of this, I often operated from a place of projection, meaning: Before I understood that *I was responsible for fixing myself*, I wanted *someone to fix me*, therefore, I subconsciously attached myself to men who needed fixing and tried to do for them what I silently wished someone to do for me. Such a mess, I know, **but this is why inner work is so important**. Identifying such a major problem definitely made me cringe, but confronting it for exactly what it was helped to change my life for the better.
The more work I did on myself, the stronger I became, and the stronger I became, the more aligned with myself and my spirit I became.

Inner work isn't something you do once then you're forever good—no. Inner work is something that you practice every day so that you can do it for the rest of your life and be great at it. My aunt was spot on:

No one is responsible for fixing anyone but themselves.

True story

It's not always only about cleaning up the people and things around us.
Sometimes, it's really all about *cleaning up inside of ourselves.*
We're not above having our own toxic traits that need to be expelled you know.

Dear Diary

I make shit hard for myself.

I know when a *situation* doesn't feel right, when a *person* doesn't feel right—but I stay around for them both. Why do I sacrifice my own mental, emotional and spiritual health by *ignoring my intuition* and staying around for situations and people that unapologetically hurt me, drain me, exhaust and drag me?

I make shit hard for myself…
and it's time to stop.

Like a Boss

Don't ever be afraid to let someone know that you are not to be played with or taken advantage of.
There's nothing cocky about straightening up your back, looking someone dead in the eyes and saying, "No, see… you got me fucked up."

It's called: ***Knowing your boundaries and respecting them.***

Stay woke

I have experienced many lows and highs in my life, and something I began noticing amidst both extremes was how certain people around me reacted to them.
You see, when I was low, *all* of my "friends" were there for me. But whenever I started to rise and it looked like I was about to hit a high, those same "friends" were rarely ever there to cheer me on, genuinely.

At first I thought that I may have been reading too much into it, so I began making excuses on behalf of my so-called friends who were missing in action—people get busy, people are dealing with their own life shit, etc. But as time went on and my high moments started becoming more frequent, the behavioural patterns of my so-called friends became harder and harder to keep making excuses for.

That's why nowadays I always say:

Pay attention to people who are *only* there for you when you're down and out, venting and crying, but when you're *up*, thriving and accomplishing all of the things you've set your heart on are quick to change the subject and/or don't really come around you.

Those people ain't your real friends, boo.

Adieu

The only people who are allowed to be close to me, are those who know how to reciprocate positive vibes and energies.

I've called too many people my "friends" only to find out, on their end, they were secretly praying for me to fail, all in the name of jealousy…

what the fuck.

See, I pray and root for my friends to win, genuinely, even when they're doing better than me.

I can't relate to jealous energies that consume some peoples bodies,
because I know that I work hard for my shit,
and what is meant for me, will always be…

for me.

"When you know better, you do better", is what I respond to people who ask me about those I've cut out of my life, purposely.

It took me a minute, but eventually I learned:

A jealous friend is not my friend at all…

that's my fucking enemy.

Lanes

Just because you see someone succeeding in a specific lane, it doesn't mean that lane is for you.

When I started publishing books and people in my city learned that I was able to quit my job and write full-time, all of a sudden, everyone and their mama's wanted to be an author, and they all came to me to ask how I did it. Now, I'm a pretty transparent human, and I don't believe in withholding information of that nature because I really believe *there's room for everyone.*
You want to write a book? You want to be a full-time author? Sweet! I'll tell you exactly how I did it, step by step, and I won't leave anything out. Putting someone else on doesn't take away from what I've got going on in the slightest, and more than that, I genuinely love seeing other people win out here—especially women.

Furthermore, when I was starting out and trying to figure out how to do all of this, no one helped me! I remember reaching out to all of the authors on the Gram who were doing their thing and not one of them responded (not that they had to, or owed me a response at all), but my point is, I know that I would have *loved* the guidance from someone who was already doing it, therefore, whenever someone asks me how I did this, I tell them.

So, I went ahead and spoon-fed everything that I had learned on my own to everyone who asked, while I simultaneously continued doing my own thing (writing, building a name for myself on social media, publishing books, etc.). Slowly but surely, *aalll* of the people who wanted to be authors out of the blue began falling off their projects one by one. Books in the making didn't get past the first ten to fifteen pages, Instagram pages they were building to market their books once finished became ghost towns, and a couple of these people even began to grow angry with me because they couldn't understand how I was able to "write so easily", "pump out books" and build my audience through my IG page at the speed that I was, and they weren't. Even though I was literally only doing for myself exactly what I had taught them… they grew angry with me. Here's the thing:

The reason why I was, and am still able to do all those things, successfully, is because

this is my dream that I had been chasing for years. I've been writing full-blown stories complete with colourful scenery and characters with extensive dialogue since I was a child. I've wanted to become a successful author since I read my first young adult book from fucking Scholastic. Writing was something that had always come natural to me; I never had to force it or think about it… I simply wrote. This is *my* dream, I was *determined* to turn it into a reality, and I was *passionate* about it.
When it came to me building my platform on social media (Instagram) and marketing my books, I've always had a very strong work ethic, and more than that… I love the hustle. The learning curves, trial and error, knowing that the possibilities are endless and there are no caps on them—all that shit is thrilling to me.

All of that said, it only made sense that my determination and love for the hustle, combined with my love, passion, and knack for writing was going to propel me into a lane that was meant for me. If being a full-time author was meant for everyone, then everyone would be a full-time, writing their asses off author; but it's not, and that's okay!

So, again… Just because you see someone succeeding in a specific lane, that doesn't mean that lane is also for you.
Never use your energy to be mad and/or salty towards someone who's succeeding. Instead, use your energy to focus on what *you are good at and are passionate about*, and let it propel you into your own lane.

Blessed & highly favoured, bitch

Sometimes I have to take a step back and realize that some people just honestly aren't worth my energy.

I'm sorry that the devil has his teeth in you, sis, and is using you to recruit; but God holds my hand every day, all day, so no…

y'all can't have me.

Shit vs Bullshit

There's a difference between putting up with someone's shit and putting up with someone's bullshit.

Someone's shit: Never knows what they want to eat, late for everything, leaves the toilet seat up, is forgetful as fuck, often has their heads in the clouds, procrastinates as fuck, etc.

Someone's bullshit: Constantly puts you down, throws you under the bus at every opportunity, forever dismisses your feelings, belittles you, never apologizes for a gawt damn thing they do and manage to make everything your fault, etc.

None of us are perfect, so we all come with our own fair share of shit. But some people come with *actual bullshit* that they refuse to acknowledge, and no one has to or should put up with that bullshit. Period.

Sound on

We are not wallowing in self-pity anymore. We are not remaining stagnant while we complain about not having the things we say we want anymore.

We are not crying about deserving better while we do nothing to obtain better.

No, ma'am.

We are getting honest with ourselves. We are getting back in touch with ourselves. We are moving, learning, and purging all the toxins we need to purge so that we can begin creating better environments for ourselves.

When we let go of the bad shit, we make room for the good shit. Good men exist. Good homegirls exist. Supporting, loving, healthy and honest circles of people exist, but we won't ever experience them if we continue to hold onto the bad shit; we have to let it the fuck go already.

No more accepting bad shit…

not even from ourselves.

How you speak to yourself
and what you put out into the universe
matters; so stop constantly
doubting yourself.

Swap, "What if I can't get through this?"
*for, "**I am going to get through this**"*
and watch how much of a difference
it makes in your life.

That part

I used to believe that loving a man unconditionally meant to stay with him no matter what…

Now I know better.

Love from a distance

"I hate him," my girl, Bria, huffed while picking at her nachos.
I laughed, "The lies we tell ourselves when we're sitting in front of a bowl of nachos with a broken heart."
"Matter of fact, I hate you too," she said through a smile that she couldn't contain.
"Yeah, yeah. Ou!" I raised my hand as the waiter hurried by. "S'cuse me," I said, my tone over-exaggerated and high-pitched.
He stopped in his tracks, backed up a few steps and leaned in toward me, "What can I get you, lovely lady?" *Okay, flirt!* I blushed a little then smiled as I caught Bria rolling her eyes.
"Can we get two more glasses of Pinot Noir, please? Oh, and a bottle of sparkling water for the table… please."
He nodded, then winked at me, "Right away, Miss."

"I know you ain't flirting with the damn waiter, B," sassed Bria after he was out of earshot.
"What? Dang. He's a cutie! Can't I have a little fun?"
"No, you cannot," she stated. "If I'm mad and sad, *we're* mad and sad. That's how

friendship works. Get in formation, B." She gulped down the last of her Pinot and I busted out laughing. "Shut *uuup,*" I told her, and she laughed too.

"He is cute though," she agreed.

"Right?! *Sweet thang.*"

She eyed me, "But he looks hella young. Lemme find out you're ready to be a cougar, B."

"Why I gotta be a cougar? Men can date women younger than them, but women can't? Fuck outta here with that mess."

She shrugged her shoulders, "I don't make the rules, B. I just deliver them."

"You ain't shit, Bria."

"*Faaaacts*," she sang, nodding her head. More laughter between us erupted as the cute waiter came back with our wine and sparkling water. He set the water down in the middle of the table, then refilled our wine glasses for us. "Thank you very much," I told him.

He bowed, "You are most welcome. I'm at your service."

"Don't tell B that," Bria blurted, "She gon' have you servicing some other *thangs* if you're not careful." I blushed extra hard and shot her a look that said, *"bitch??"*, but the waiter only smiled.

"Like I said," he started, looking at her then turning back to me, "I am at your service."

• • •

After he walked away, I kicked her under the table, causing her to almost spill the fresh glass of wine that she was holding up to her lips. "Aye!" she yelped through a giggle, "You brought me out to get my mind off of shit and have a good time, and *this is me* having a good time!" Then she sighed, "Thanks for taking me out though, B. For real. I needed this."
"I gotchu, you know that," I reminded her, and took a sip of my wine.
"I know you do."

She gazed off for a moment into the crowded restaurant at nothing in particular, "I don't hate him," she whispered, referring to her now ex boyfriend. "I still love him, so much. I just… I can't keep doing this shit with him anymore, you know?" She looked at me and I nodded, "Yep, I know, girl."

"For my own sanity, for my own fucking dignity, I had to leave. Yeah I still love him, but I don't want to be with him anymore. What makes me sick is all the nerve he had trying to guilt trip me, talkin' bout, *if you really loved me, then you wouldn't leave.* Can you believe that shit? And I won't even lie, that fucked with my head for a good two weeks. I kept replaying those words and asking myself, *Is he right? Do I really love him if I'm able to walk away?* But then I had to shake that shit off and come back to reality. *He* was the one treating *me* like shit for the last year, emotionally and mentally abusing me, *not the other muthafuckin' way around.* So how dare he, B? How *daaare* he? *If you really loved me then you wouldn't leave*—Muthafucka? If *you* really loved *me* then you wouldn't have treated me the way you did! Isn't that textbook emotional fucking manipulation?"

"Yep," I confirmed.

"Ugh, disgusting! He can miss the fuck outta me with that bullshit."

She sighed once more, took another sip of her wine, then ate a couple of nachos.

"These are fucking bomb by the way," she said through a full mouth and I laughed.

"I'm serious! Try some!"

I shook my head, "Nah, those things are going to have me sitting on the toilet all night. No thanks. I'm good with my calamari."

"Bougie ass bitch."

"Sure the fuck am!" I proudly beamed, raising my glass in the air.

"Anyway," she continued. "He's just not worth it anymore. I guess I'm finally coming to terms with that."

"I completely feel you," I said, popping a piece of calamari into my mouth. "At the end of the day, girl, we all need to remember that the love that we have for someone isn't measured by how much abuse we're willing to take from them. We can love the entire fuck out of someone from a far distance if it means protecting our well being."

"Well shit, bitch. Can we toast to that real muthafuckin' quick? See, this is why you were born to be a writer. Look at you! Look at the shit you say! Like, that was a *whole word.* Actually, no, *that is a mantra*. You better write that down and put it in a book somewhere." I smiled as we lifted our glasses and toasted. "To protecting our well being," she said.
"To protecting our well being," I repeated. After setting her glass down, she reached for some more nachos, "I'm serious by the way. Write that shit down, like now, so you don't forget it… then put it in a book."
I laughed, "Alright, alright. You right!" I took my phone out, opened the "notes" section and jotted it down.

Free your mind

Stop letting these ain't shit,
don't have a pot of their own to piss in,
need to depend on you for everything dudes
manipulate your brain into thinking you
need them, when actually…

it's *the other way around.*

It starts with you

"He needs to start respecting me."
"He needs to start treating me better."
No, sis. *You* need to start *respecting yourself* by implementing *boundaries* and not allowing him, or anyone else for that matter, to continuously disrespect you.
You need to start *setting examples* for people by *treating yourself better*, and part of that means revoking access from anyone who treats you badly to begin with.

Serving hot tea

Don't let anyone guilt trip you
for having not waited around for them
to change their shitty ass, problematic
behaviour.

You don't owe anyone years of your life
in exchange for the decline of your
mental and emotional health.

Dodged bullets

Many years ago when shit finally hit the fan with my then emotionally, mentally and a couple of times physically abusive boyfriend, and I was leaving his ass for good, his baby mother said to me: "Girl, you don't even know how lucky you are. You get to walk away from this man and never look back, but because I have a child with him… I have to deal with him for the rest of my life."

And until this very day, anytime I'm reflecting on all of the bullets I've dodged throughout my life, I remember her words like they were yesterday… and I get the chills. Then I bow my head and thank God that I never had a child with that guy.

What you need to hear

I remember back when I was in my early twenties, heartbroken over some guy who I had broken up with. I was over at my aunt's house telling her the story as I cried my eyes out. She looked at me and said, "You can be anything you want to be in this world, and yet, you're choosing to be the girl who spends her Saturday nights crying over some piece of shit who doesn't care about her at all… now *this* is sad."

Now that I'm older we laugh about that moment often because…

she was right.

Give it to them straight

"Don't tell me I'm asking for too fucking much," I told him, furiously. "Say that you don't want to. Say you don't know how. Say you don't have it in you. Say any-fucking-thing-else but don't you ever tell me that I'm asking for too much. You're allowed to have shortcomings, be afraid, have commitment issues, not be interested in me in that type of way, or still want to play the field—I *can't* and *won't* hold any of those things against you. But I won't allow you to flip shit and make it seem like I'm abnormal for wanting something real, simply because you aren't the man who *can* or *wants* to give it to me."

Curtains closed

Let me tell you how he *thought* this was
gonna go:

He'd say, "Let me explain," and I'd fold my
arms across my chest, maybe roll my eyes
but respond, "Fine, I'm listening—go."

He'd then proceed to talk his talks,
using carefully chosen words
to ensure that I would remain calm.
Because while he wants me to understand
where he's coming from,
he also wants to make it clear
that he already knows
he was dead ass wrong.

And after letting it all out,
and apologizing for all of his lies
he'd then swear that it would never
happen again
while staring directly at me,
sincerity bleeding from his eyes.

And I'd believe him, say I understand him,
then he'd pull me close and hold me tight.
And while I'd probably resist a bit, at first,
he'll count on me giving in just like I have
every other time—right?

Now let me tell you how that shit *really*
went down:

It didn't.
I'm no one's fool anymore.
And before his little play could even start,
I exited stage left
without making so much as a sound.

Dear Diary part 2

I'm legitimately at a point in my life where I've realized that offering the words, "It's complicated" to describe a relationship is utter bullshit.

We're either dating, or we're not.
We're either committed to each other, or we're not. We're either breathing life into each other, or we're not.
There is no reason why a relationship, in any capacity, has to be complicated. We're either on the same page, moving forward in a manner that is fair to the both of us…

or we're fucking not.

Fix UP

Stop waiting for the dude you're with to change.

You gon' fuck around and wake up ten years later exhausted, jaded, bitter and mad that *you spent some of the best years of your life waiting on a man who never changed, anyway*. Get your self-love levels up so that your self-esteem can follow, because low self-esteem will have you staying with men who not only treat you poorly, but also confuse you and have you believing that it's better to have them than no one at all.

Fix up, baby girl. Fix UP.

Cut the cord

Be it a relationship that you've been in for a long ass time with a lover, or a friendship that you've had for a long ass time with a homegirl—*sometimes it's just time to cut the damn cord.*
Whether the relationship/friendship has become toxic as fuck, or you merely find yourself no longer having any common ground—*dead weight is dead weight.*

I used to hold onto certain people who I knew I didn't belong around anymore, all because I was holding onto the memories of what we *used to be*.
The fun we *used to have.*
The way we *used to be able to communicate.*
The way we *used to hang out.*
The *same page we used to be on.*

Once I stopped looking at them through memories of the past and began seeing them through the present, shit became crystal clear: *I still have mad love for you, but it's time to go our separate ways.*

Miss me, literally

"I miss the old you," he said, and I shook my head. "Of course you miss the old me; why wouldn't you? That girl was broken and spiritually disconnected, therefore, accepted all kinds of shit from you. Always let you back in whenever you felt like coming back and constantly betrayed her own boundaries. Of course you miss her as you stand here listening to the new me rebuke the entire shit out of you, and all of the toxicities that come with you. The new me doesn't appeal to you, and why would she? You don't like women who love themselves."

A peaceful woman

For some men, the definition of "a peaceful woman" is one who caters to their wants and needs and never "annoys" them with her own, never confronts or questions them about anything, and stays loyal to them while they sleep around.

My advice to every woman in the world:
You want to be a peaceful woman?
Then stay the entire fuck away from these types of men.

Permission granted

You are allowed to want better for yourself if you're with someone who is abusive in any way—be it mentally, verbally, emotionally, physically—or all the mentioned combined.
You're allowed to close the door on anyone who is wreaking havoc on your mind, body, spirit, soul and heart, and never open it to them again.

Self-fucking-Love

In the past, I've given a few ain't shit men way too many ego boosts by staying with them. Rewarding their constant cheating, lying, disrespect and every other shitty thing they did by giving them stability, loyalty, faithfulness, home-cooked meals, vagina and comfort.

See why self-love is so fucking vital?

When you know better

I have an ex who I was with for about three years. The first year was roses and sunshine, but by the third year he was emotionally and verbally abusive as fuck.
When I left him, he said, “No one is ever going to love you the way that I do.”
I had to chuckle before responding,

“Buddy… this *isn’t* love.”

Mic check

Think about all of the energy and effort you've put into trying to get some dude who treats you like you're garbage to see that you aren't. Sis? Take all of that same energy and effort, put it into yourself and *flourish the fuck away from him.*

Smarten up

"Baby girl," she said.
"You can't expect a man
who lies to himself every day
to be honest with you."

Level up only

Every time I've ever decided to give someone a small taste of their own medicine after they've hurt me, repeatedly, it's only backfired, making me feel even worse than I did to begin with. That was God reminding me that I am not them and had no business stooping to their levels.

This is why I'm never interested in getting revenge, but instead, always interested in moving the fuck on with my life.

Wanting to have your feelings
spared and coddled all the time
will never get you anywhere.
Surround yourself with women
who love you enough
to keep it all the way real with you.

Self-fucking-care

We cannot attach ourselves to men who we've already recognized as ***emotionally unavailable***, make them our entire world, then blame them for draining us of everything we had to give.
Part of self-care is understanding that anyone who is unavailable in any capacity, means—*not for us.*
If a man has shown us who he is and we don't like it, that's *our* cue to dip.

Cheers

The hostess of the Ritz Carlton Hotel led me through the dinning area and over to the bar where my girl, Angel, was already seated with a cocktail in front of her. “Okay, fine like a glass of proper wine!” she sang as she spotted me sashaying my way over.
I thanked the hostess before she walked away, then sat down on the plush bar chair beside Angel. “I ain’t the only fine wine here,” I winked, referring to her.
She batted her eyelashes and smacked her lips together, “Well, you know how we do.”
The bartender presented himself and offered me a cocktail menu, alongside a food menu.
“Hi,” I greeted, “I actually don’t need any of the menus, I’ll have a Hennessy and ginger ale.” He nodded, “Right away, Mademoiselle.

“Whoa?” Angel eyed me suspiciously. “B? Not eating? Drinking Henny over champagne or red wine? Uh, uh, bitch. What’s going on?” That’s the thing about real friends—they know you better than you know yourself sometimes. I loved food and never turned down an opportunity to eat, and if I wasn’t in a club atmosphere, I for sure wasn’t drinking no damn Hennessy. So for me for me to have an appetite for *Henny* instead of *food?* Something was definitely wrong with me.

“Girl,” I began, but before I could continue, Erika’s voice rang out through the restaurant, “Who let the dogs out?!”
“*Who, who, who, who, who*?” Jazzy sang behind her as backup.
“It’s woof, Jazzy. *Woof, woof, woof, woof, woof*,” Erika corrected her and Jazzy kissed her teeth, “Lemme sing the song the way I want to sing it! Shit.”
Everyone seated in our area turned to look at who was making all the commotion, and Angel and I shook our heads. “Can’t take these bitches no damn place,” she muttered, smirking. The hostess’s face turned a little red as she led them to us, and I chuckled lightly.

Erika and Jazzy flung their arms around me, dramatically, and hugged me tight. “Can y’all get the fuck off me?” I asked through a laugh. They knew I wasn’t a big hugger, so they liked to fuck with me.
“What kind of a Pisces doesn’t like hugs?” Jazzy, who was also a Pisces, quizzed as she rolled her eyes jokingly.
“The type who has Aquarius as her rising sign,” I answered, “Now get the *hell* off of

me." We all shared a laugh as Jazzy and Erika let go of me and took their seats.

"Nice to see everyone lookin' *flyyy*," acknowledge Erika.
"When do we ever *not* look fly?" Angel asked.
"We're The Too Fly crew!" Jazzy said, and Angel shook her head, "Can we have one day of you not being corny?"
Jazzy sighed, putting a hand on her hip, "It's a tough job, but someone has to do it."
I high-fived Jazzy's free hand as we all laughed again.
"Hennessy and ginger ale," the bartender interrupted, placing the drink in front of me.
"Oh… *Hold up*," Erika said looking at my drink, then at me, then at all of us. "This is an intervention for B? 'Cause I definitely didn't get the memo."
Angel tapped her long fingernails along the marble bar, "Girl, you and me both."

"It's not an intervention, y'all," I told them.
"Lies," Angel quipped.
"Shit. Henny for all of us then," Jazzy turned to the bartender and ordered.

Once we all had our drinks and had taken our first sips, Erika spoke up, "*Sooo*, you gon' tell us why you're mad, B? Or nah?"

"I'm not mad, I'm just…"
Angel cut me off, "Bitch, you mad. Okay?" You sittin' here ordering Henny at 8pm on a damn Tuesday. You mad!" I shook my head and sighed, "Fine. I *am* mad," I confessed. "I'm mad, I'm annoyed, I'm sad… I'm a bunch of low vibrational emotions right now."

"What the hell happened?" Jazzy asked.
"What bitch we gotta fight?" Erika added, which made me laugh.
"We ain't fighting no-flippin-body. Damn, Erika? Why you always tryna beat someone up?"
She shrugged, "Jazzy's job is to say corny shit, dress in fly name-brand fits from head to toe and be compassionate, yours is to be the mediator and keep it real, but still be sensitive at the same time, and mine is to organize shit and ride or die for my girls—which includes fighting a bitch. Any other questions?"
Angel raised an eyebrow, "Uh, excuse the fuck outta me? So I ain't got no jobs round here?"
"To be the smart-mouth whose hair is always laid, makeup always slayed and drive the getaway car," Jazzy answered.

"Ah *shiiieet*. Set it off in this *biiiitch*!" Angel sang raising her glass, and we all busted out laughing.
"I *cannot* stand y'all," I said, then proceeded to fill them in on what happened.

"So, okay. I'm laying in my bed this morning, minding the business that pays me. I open my Instagram, pop into my DM's and to my fucking shock, was met with this…" I unlocked my phone and began reading from the screenshot I had taken:

"Cici? B? Whatever it is they call you, I just wanted to make a few things crystal clear to you.
1. Whatever little fun you and Stephan had is dead. He's MY man, get over it.
2. Don't contact him again, for anything.
3. You can stop writing your little quotes about him as well. Everyone can feel your jealousy in every word, and hey, I'd be jealous of me too if I were you. After all, at the end of the day I'M the one he claims as his woman, and I'M the one he takes care of.

Last but not least, there are plenty of other men in the sea, sweetie. I suggest you go fishing for your own."

"See, this is why I stay ready to fight a bitch," Erika said through gritted teeth. "Run me her address, 'cause she got you FUCKED up."

"Why do women do this?" Jazzy asked. "Like, is she slow or what? You *didn't know* he had a girlfriend until you *found out* he had a girlfriend *and* a bunch of other girls in his rotation. The fuck is wrong with her? She needs to take that shit up with his triflin' ass, not you!"

"She ain't his girlfriend," Angel corrected. "After everything we found out about Stephan and all of the other chicks he has, she ain't his girlfriend—she's his safety-net, his plan Z."

None of us could hold back our giggles.

"Leave it to Angel to call the girl a plan Z," said Jazzy.

"What? It's the truth! She's what he runs back to when all his other chicks are giving him a headache, and by headache, I mean kicking his ass to the curb when they find out he's a triflin' ass hoe and blocking him from everywhere. *A plan muthafuckin' Z.*" She took a long sip of her drink, then motioned the bartender to bring over another round.

"Don't let that chick get to you, B," Jazzy reasoned. "I know you really liked Stephan, and finding out about her and all the others really hit you hard, but don't let her fuck with your head. She has it worse than you when you think about it."
"I did really like him," I admitted, staring at my drink. "Like, was this close to falling in love with him type of liked him, and this shit threw me all the way off. Damn near a whole year of being in each other's faces every day and night, I still just don't understand how he even had time for other women, let alone have a whole girlfriend hidden in the shadows. Like, where was she? When did they even see each other? Shit just doesn't make sense."

"Plan Z," Angel reminded me. "And that's how these good for nothing but some dick, tongue and a stick of bubble gum men roll out here. They're calculated. Strategic. They know how to play their game. Just be glad you didn't fuck around and get knocked up by him." I felt my eyes begin to water, and I put my palms to my forehead. "Okay, no, *nooooo*," she scolded. "We're not doing none of this crying shit, especially not at the Ritz fucking Carlton, and especially not over piece of shit Stephan! Pull it together, B."

She was right. I pulled myself together before any tears could make their escape, took a deep breath and downed the rest of my drink right as a new one was placed in front of me.

"Run me her address, B," Erika demanded once more, fuming.
"No, Erika," huffed Jazzy, "You can't be out here fighting the girl when *she isn't the problem.*"
Erika looked at her as if she had lost her mind, "I'm sorry, are we in different conversations here? Was it not the *girl* who fixed her audacious ass fingers to message B with this foolery, when B was minding her own fucking business and already cut all communication with Stephan? And was it not the *girl* who had the fucking cheek to think she could tell B what she could and could *not* write about, *and* call her jealous? Nah, sounds like *she's* the fucking problem to me."
Irritated, Jazzy shook her head, "Your hot-headed ass is gonna land you in a jail cell one of these days, Erika."
Erika shrugged her shoulders and grinned, "And y'all heffa's finna be there to bail me out! Duh! Specifically, B, since she's making the big author bucks now." She

winked at me and I couldn't help but grin while I shook my head.

"This is why both y'all asses are single. Spend all your damn time arguing with each other like an old married couple," Angel interjected.

Jazzy gasped, "Rude!" and we all cracked up.

"I'm not running you her address, Erika," I finally said. "Thank you for always being ready to literally drag a bitch, but Jazzy is right. That girl isn't the problem, *he* is, and she *is* the one with the shittiest end of the stick. All of us have been the plan Z at some point or another in our lives. Some of us for a week, some for a few years, but we all know what that shit is like, nonetheless. I mean, shit… remember James? I was definitely his plan Z and I let myself be that. Why? Because I had no concept of self-love."

All of my girls nodded as they remembered my most notorious shitshow of a relationship several years back, then reflected on their own past experiences as "plan Z's".

"Why must you and Jazzy always have to make sense?" Erika asked, rolling her eyes playfully.

"Just doing our *jobs*," Jazzy winked, and we all smiled at each other.
"Sometimes I hate making sense though," I admitted. "I wanted to cuss her the fuck out *soooo* bad when I wrote her back. Like, read her for absolute filth… but I didn't."

"Wait a hot damn minute now," Angel blurted out. "You wrote her back?" I nodded. "Well shit, bitch! Let us hear what you said!"
I took another sip of my drink, then unlocked my phone again and began reading my response:

"Sis, I'll be painfully honest with you. A younger, less knowledgeable version of myself would have definitely felt some type of way about all of that, hands down. But the woman that I am today knows better... so much better. I can assure you that any man who "claims you", but carries on romantic relationships with a plethora of other women every night he feels like it is nothing for me to be jealous of. More than that, the fact that you think him having you out here looking like a damn fool is "taking care of you" makes me want to wrap my arms around you and give you the tightest hug you've ever had.

I'm sorry that you're going through what you're going through, and that you feel like you have to save face by accusing me and who knows how many other women of being jealous. Some of us eventually wake up, some of us never do, but I hope that one day you do wake up and become a better, more knowledgeable version of yourself, too. Take care of yourself."

I looked up at my girls and shrugged my shoulders, "And that's that."

"You know what, B? I'm fucking proud of you," Erika said.
"Same," Jazzy and Angel agreed.
"And honestly," Jazzy continued, "That response *was* a read, but it was the type of read that probably hit her right in her conscious, and is going to be one that plays in her mind over and over again until the day she finally leaves his ass… if she ever does, that is."
"True muthafuckin' story," approved Angel.

I tapped my stiletto shaped fingernails against my glass, "Yeah… I guess. I mean, I know I did the right thing, 'cause I can feel that I did the right thing. I guess I'm just upset at the situation in its entirety. Know what I mean? Like, her mentions of my writing didn't bother me 'cause I own everything that I've been through, therefore, I can write whatever the fuck I want, and her calling me jealous was literally just her projecting—so all of that is whatever. I'm just mad at dudes like Stephan and fed up of watching women like her *let* these types of men run their fucking lives. I should have sent her a copy of Letters to My Ex." I took the last sip of my drink while making eye contact with the bartender. He gave me the, "another round?" look, which I returned with the "Yes, please" look.

Angel nodded, "Girl, you ain't neva lied. But whatever, like you said to her, hopefully she wakes the fuck up but until then, she's gonna keep putting up with his shit. As for him, *he ain't shit* and karma's gonna catch him when he least expects it—it's always like that. You kicked his ass out of your life now, so don't give his shit any more energy. You didn't waste your time with him because you learned something from this whole mess, but if you keep giving it energy now that it's over, then you're the one wasting your own damn time."
I screwed my face up at her, "And what did I learn from this shit, Angel?"

"To post a picture of the next dude you start seeing, and if no one claims him in twenty-four hours… you may proceed," she smirked and raised her glass.

"You're a damn fool!" I laughed, and everyone else did too. "Who needs men when we have our girlfriends?" Jazzy beamed, and Angel raised her palm towards her, "Okay, no, bitch. Don't get ahead of yourself 'cause last *I* checked, *I* need them for that *dick* and *so do the rest of y'all*. Shit. Just gotta find the dicks that are attached to the good men of the world, that's all."

More laughter rang out between the four of us, and after we gathered ourselves, I shook my head, "I'm hungry, now. Y'all tryna fuck up some oysters and a steak, or what?"

"*Shiiiiet*, B's back!" Erika cheered.

"Amen to that!" Jazzy joined and waved her hand to get the bartender's attention.

"Oh, by the way," Angel turned to face me, "Did she ever respond to your message?"

I smiled mischievously, "You know me better than that. I say what I have to say, then I'm out. Block game hella strong." I raised my glass as she smiled and raised hers, "That's my B. Cheers."

The high road

Fighting another woman over a serial cheating ass man is only showing that man he's worth the fight, when in reality, he isn't. Community dick is always going to do its job—serve the community.
A woman with self-love will do her job—serve her dignity and self-respect by seeing herself out of the community she doesn't want to be apart of.

The other foot

"I get that it hurts," I told my girl.
"Obviously when you fall in love with someone you'd like for them to love you back; but I think it's so important to remind ourselves that nobody owes us love. For instance, how many times has a guy been desperately head over heels for you, but you simply didn't feel the same way?"
She thought for a second, then answered, reluctantly, "Many times."
"And did the fact that you simply didn't feel the same way make you a bad person, even though it hurt his feelings?" I asked.
"No."
"Exactly," I said. "It wasn't that you were a piece of shit, a player, a bitch, or trying to hurt him. You were getting to know a guy, he fell in love and you didn't. So now that the shoe is on *your* foot and you've fallen in love with a guy who doesn't feel the same way about you, why do you have to paint him out to be some kind of monster?"

She toyed with the handle of her coffee mug, processing my words. "I… I don't know. Guess I've never really thought of it like that."

“Again, I know it hurts,” I continued. “You *know* I do. But there’s a difference between a painful situation, and a person who deliberately causes you pain; and I think we’ve all been guilty, at some point, of allowing whatever pain we’re feeling from a rejection to stop us from realizing the difference between the two.”

He's not ready...

If a guy says, "I really like you, but I'm not ready to be in a relationship right now", but *you* are ready to be in a relationship with someone, sis…

This is not the time for you to get out your read between the lines starter kit and try to figure out what he "really means".
Some things *are* truly *black or white*, and this is one of those things. So, *what he really means* is exactly what the hell he just said— a relationship is not something he's interested in. Period.

This is also definitely not the time to take him saying that he isn't ready to be in a relationship as a CHALLENGE for you to try to change his mind by staying "loyal" and "faithful" to him.
"Bet once he sees how ride or die I am, he won't want to let me go. Shit, I'm wifey material, and he's gonna realize that."— Um, full fucking stop, sis. Abort the entire shit out of that dumb ass mission because this is how we end up breaking our own hearts! We end up spending *months,* and sometimes even *years* in imaginary ass relationships with these men all because *we*

decided to promote ourselves to the title of their girlfriends, all the while they aren't our boyfriends. Then, when something drastic happens and smacks us out of the la-la land *we created*, we turn around and blame them. Read that last paragraph again! I've been there, done that before, and it's not cute.

If you know that you want to be in a committed, monogamous relationship with someone, but the guy you're dating/seeing has said flat out that **he doesn't want that for himself**, then it is your responsibility to exit stage left, sis. No if's, and's, but's or imaginary shit about it. *"Hey, this has been fun and I'm really enjoying you, but we are in different places in our lives. I'm looking for a commitment and you're not—which is fine, I respect it—but before I get caught up and my feelings for you get any stronger, I'm gonna have to end this here."*

And, yes, **it is that simple.**

Self-love will make a lot of the shit you have been so accustomed to calling "complicated" **that simple**. How? Because amongst many others, one of the things under the umbrella of self-love is self-respect; and when you respect yourself, you don't settle for people who aren't on the same page as you. You don't suppress or ignore your needs all in the name of being able to say you have a man in your life. You don't lie to yourself, and *you respect where other people are in their lives, too.*

It's okay if a guy you're dating/seeing doesn't want the same thing(s) as you; rather than trying to *make* him change his mind, *let go* so that *you* can make space in your mind, heart, soul, spirit and *life* for someone else to come along who does.

Do you, boo

I stopped giving ultimatums to people I have relationships with—friends, lovers, and family members alike.
I don't even know when I stopped, exactly, but what I do remember was thinking to myself, *"If someone I have a relationship with begins to behave in a way that directly and negatively affects my peace and I, and are aware because I've communicated that to them a few times, yet are quite comfortable continuing to behave in that manner, regardless… then it's because that's what they want to do. Therefore, why would I want to force anyone to change what they're comfortable doing, when I can simply remove myself from their life and return to the peace I worked hard to create in my own life?"*

Problem solved as fuck.

Solo trips

"My homegirl is with a man who treats her horribly," wrote a woman in my comment section on Instagram one day. "And not only do I feel like a broken record from repeating the same things to her, over and over again, every time she comes to me for advice, but her issues are starting to take a toll on me."

Her comment resonated with me deeply because I knew exactly how she felt, so I responded, "You wanna know what I've learned about people once I began to study myself and the old versions of myself? You cannot make anyone understand a muthafuckin' thing. It just is what it is. I always revert back to the old saying, *"You can lead a horse to water, but you can't make it drink."*

Your homegirl is where many of us have been before—low on self-love. You can try to fill her cup all you want, but ultimately, it's something she's going to have to truly want to fill for herself. Feel me? I understand you in my SOUL when you say, "I can't handle this anymore" because that shit is draining for you, a thousand percent. I had to learn with my experiences with friends like this to put up boundaries for

myself because I have the right to protect my emotional and mental health, too. So I would say to my friends, *"Listen, I love you with my everything, but I cannot help you until you actively want to help yourself. I'm here for you, but not at the expense of my own mental and emotional health, and that's exactly what this is becoming."*
Loving people from a distance is a real thing, and sometimes, that's just what it takes. We all have our paths we have to travel in life, and sometimes, some of those paths are dark and we have to travel them alone. Why? So that we can learn how to find our own light within ourselves.
Maybe, just maybe, this is the time when your homegirl has to find her own light within."

"Be with someone who makes you happy."

No, sis.

Learn how to create happiness
within yourself,
then be with someone who adds to it.

Wave buh-bye

If you're the woman who is always crying and unhappy because you're forever taking everyone's bullshit, try switching it up and practice taking *no one's* bullshit.
You claim that you want peace in your life, you beg for it while you pray at night, yet you continue to make excuses for the problematic people who you allow to stay around you, and the toxic man who you keep allowing inside of you.
Come on, now… make it make sense.
At this point, what do you have to lose?
People who don't care about you?

That's a great thing, sis—*lose them.*

Be about yourself

"Be about yourself, girl," I told her.
"Your goals, your ambitions, your mental, emotional and spiritual health, your growth, your paper. You've already been about the toxic shit. The low frequency shit. The focusing on the men who didn't give a fuck about you shit. The spending every second night crying yourself to sleep, then calling into work sick because it—fucking up your paper shit. The circle of friends who weren't even your true friends shit.
The lying to yourself shit. The putting everyone else's wants and needs above your own, prioritizing the wrong shit, shit.
You've been there, done that, and what has it brought you?" She stayed silent as a tear fell from her eye. "Exactly," I continued.
"Nothing but a domino effect of…"
"Bullshit," she interjected, finishing the sentence as she wiped her tear away.
I nodded, "Right. So come on, now. You owe it to yourself to *be about yourself*."

Fruit Tree

I had just broken it off with my dude. He hadn't done anything necessarily bad to me, like, he didn't cheat, disrespect me or violate my boundaries or anything like that. I broke it off with him because I was meeting all of his needs, while there were far too many of mine that he was not meeting. Of course, before I made the decision to end it, I had a conversation with him and explained in detail how I was feeling; and I must say, he was all ears. There is something extremely soothing about being able to experience a man who listens to the valid concerns and feelings you bring to his attention, and rather than trying to invalidate them by gaslighting the entire shit out of you, takes full accountability. I say it's soothing because, regardless of the fact that he and I didn't work out in the end, it proves that men like that do exist.

By the end of our conversation, he made it very clear that he would do better, and I was hopeful. Exactly one month later, however, absolutely *nothing* had changed, and on the morning of July 21st, I was literally awoken out of my sleep by my intuition yelling,

"You gave a shot, good for you, he ain't the one though, so… free yourself."
I shit you not, I sat up in my bed and before I even brushed my teeth, I sent him a three-minute voice-note saying that nothing had changed, I had needs that he obviously wasn't capable of meeting and that I was ending this.

As I sat on my bed reflecting on what I had just done, I felt proud of myself; but at the same time felt frustrated as fuck.
There I was—this beautiful, loving, understanding, supportive, open-minded, open-spirited, hardworking, accomplished, fun, bubbly, playful, good ass fucking woman who was ready for a *partner* in life and *healthy* love. I was ready for someone who brought just as much to the table as I did, but it was beginning to feel as though I was shooting for the fucking stars.
Remember when Charlotte from Sex and the City said, "I've been dating since I was fifteen. I'm exhausted. Where is he?"—
Okay, BIG MOOD.

Bria, my best friend of twelve years just so happened to have called me right in the middle of my contradicting feelings to ask for my opinion on something she was dealing with. After listening to her dilemma and giving my opinion, she then asked me how I was doing. I sighed. A deep, long, extra as fuck sigh, "Blah. I broke it off with Dwight,"

"Shit, eh? I saw that coming, though," She said. "After the whole needs not being met thing you told me about last month, yeah… I know you, B. You weren't about to stay with him."

"*Uuugghhhhhh*," I moaned. "You have emotional and mental space along with some time for a vent?" I asked her.

"Yep! Let it out, girly. Let it *ouuuut*."

Shit, she didn't have to tell me twice! Everything that was sitting at the top of my throat chakra came pouring out.

"Like, you'd think I was out here asking men to buy me a private jet the way they cannot get with a simple fucking program. Meet my needs, fam! I give out that ol' school R&B type of lovin' when I'm with a man, and gawt damn it, I need it the fuck back from him. Give me flowers just because. Shoot me a, "I'm thinking of you," text in the middle of the afternoon. Randomly tell me that I'm beautiful. It doesn't matter that I already know I'm beautiful, nor does it matter that random men tell me that shit all day—I don't give fuck about them. *You're my man*, I want to hear that shit from you! The same way I, "You're so handsome" you to death and make you feel desired and wanted by me, I want to feel the same way. Like, the fuck? Light some candles around the kitchen table, even if we've ordered in. Plan a weekend getaway, even if it's only an hour away. Stand outside my house with a fucking boom-box playing, "I'll Make Love to You" by Boyz II Men or something; I don't know! But do shit to romance me, and keep doing shit to romance me throughout our relationship because I do shit to romance you! All the shit that these new-age chicks have the fucking nerve to call, "corny"—I love all of that. Further-the-fuck-more, why wouldn't you want to reciprocate the same good feelings your woman gives to you? Why? Why? *Whhhyyyaaaaa*?

Be affectionate, yo! Don't just bask in the constant and steady flow of affection you receive from me—GIVE IT THE FUCK BACK. Take initiative, and not just with romance and affection, but with other things, too. I'm over here quite literally running shit—I am my own whole ass publishing house… *hellooooo*? I am an authorpreneur.

I spend my days making every single decision from writing, to what gets edited, to what gets released and where—is this piece going on my IG or am I saving it for a book? *I* make these calls. I'm here deciding on book covers, fonts, formatting—do I want quotes in between each chapter, or do I just want chapter titles alone? Decisions, decisions! Let's not forget my podcast, my merch, oh, and not to mention my IG page is its whole living, breathing thing on its own that needs to be ran a very specific way. So it's like, FAM… I don't always want to be in charge of making every single decision in a relationship, too. The *fuuuuck*. A relationship is two people—two! Why do I always have to be the one to make the reservations? Why do I always have to be the one to decide if we're gonna stay in or go out? Why do I always have to be the one to decide what we're gonna eat or who's going to cook? WHY CAN'T YOUR ASS BE LIKE, "BABE… PULL OUT ONE OF THOSE SEXY LITTLE DRESSES THAT HAVE BEEN SITTING IN YOUR CLOSET FOR THE PAST TWO MONTHS

WITH THE TAGS STILL ON EM, I'M TAKING YOU OUT TONIGHT." But, no. *Neeeoooooo*. I have to be the one who is like, "HEY, BABE… GO GET A HAIRCUT, YOU'RE TAKING ME OUT TONIGHT." Jesus! I don't want to run shit in a relationship, Bria. I don't need a fucking *intern* as my man, I need a PARTNER as my man. Why is this so complicated? It's not. It shouldn't be! I don't ask for much. The shit I ask for in a relationship is the basic standard fucking shit: Have respect, know how to communicate, have some emotional intelligence, have your own income, don't stick your dick anywhere else—*these are basic, standard things, Bri*. Then when it comes to my needs to be met—they're not a fucking laundry list, either. But these men… man, *oh my gaawwwd*, these men I come across it's like, holy shit! They either meet my needs, but fall hella short when it comes to the basic standards, are excellent on the standards end, but suck at meeting my needs, or they're right in-between on both ends and it's like… WHAT IS GOING ON? Then, *theeen*, when you address the areas they're falling short in, they either, A- Get offended.

B- Gaslight you and call you crazy.

C- Say that you're too demanding and asking for way too much.

D- Fully acknowledge their shortcomings and say they're going to do better but then don't—*Dwight*.

E- Call you complicated and a nag.

Or F- My fucking favourite of all time… tell you that other women have never had a problem with them. Like, okay? SORRY YOUR OTHER WOMEN HAD HELLA LOW BARS, BITCH. The fuck?"

I paused for a few seconds to gather myself, then sighed again, "I'm just having a moment. Like, I know in my brain that this is literally just a moment of frustration. There's someone out there for me that will fit like a glove, I know there is, but holy shitballs, I don't how many more fucking frogs I can be out here kissing, Bria!"

Bria let out a laugh, "How many more frogs do I have to kiss?—A novel by, Cici. B."
I couldn't help but to laugh too, "Fuck off, Bri!"

She cleared her throat, "Okay, okay… but nah, I fucking feel you! And no, B, you're not asking for much at all, like at *alllll*. It's just these niggas, yo… they're fucking dumb and to be honest with you, B, a lot of them are intimidated by you."
I rolled my eyes, "But *whyyyy*? For what?! Shit drives me crazy. I'm just here being me! I'm giving, too fucking giving, actually. I'm open, I extend myself, I communicate hella clearly, I express, I listen—holy shit, I listen so much that I should send some of these men bills for all the fucking therapy sessions I've given. I'm always working on myself so that I can grow and rise above my own bullshit. WHAT IS THERE TO BE INTIMIDATED ABOUT?"

"But that's it, B," she jumped in. "You nailed it right there—*you're always working*. B, you're so smart. Like, when you talk, you know what the fuck you're talking about and that alone is enough for a lot of these men out here to be like, *okay, whoa… I can't keep up with this chick*.
Then, you're always working on yourself. Inner work is something that you are extremely invested in and take seriously, so you're always finding ways to educate

yourself while opening yourself up to let other educate you, too. All of this is dope by the way. Like, you're doing what you're supposed to be doing, shit, what we are *all* supposed to be doing. But… a lot of these men who get around you get intimidated by that part of you too, because watching the way *you* work, forces them to see how little they work, and in order for them to be with you for the long haul, it would mean they would have no choice but to start doing their work… and they don't want to, B.
A lot of these men out here don't want to do their fair share of work. You're not complicated, you're not asking for too much, you're not a nag, and you're not crazy; but these types of men will call you all of those things in hopes that it will break you down just enough for you to stop being *you* and shrink to their level, so that *they* can breathe easy, and no longer feel like they have to do any of their own work to rise in order to meet you at *your* level. It's fucked up, but that's exactly why these types of men don't deserve you, and never did, B."

Man, not one lie left her mouth, and fuck… those truths hit me hella hard.

It's sad, you know?

It's sad that instead of these men being inspired to do their own inner work so that they could then begin to create *healthy environments for themselves*, thus start having *healthy relationships with women*, they would rather just continue living in their own toxicities, and more than that, prey on women who don't have any boundaries, are low on self-love, etc… because they know those are the women who will call the bullshit crumbs being thrown at them "love". Those are the women who will silence, neglect and hurt themselves all in the name of keeping these specific men feeling comfortable so they don't leave them. I know, because a few versions of myself ago… *I was those women.*

It sucks because you work so hard on yourself, day in and day out, to not be those women anymore. You slowly begin to purge all the bad shit you learned from growing up in a broken home, toxic environments, etc... and begin to replace them with good shit. Your mind starts to open, and you start to become so fucking self-aware that you can call *yourself out* with no problem or hesitation when you're fucking up. Your spirit starts to open, and that shit is *magical* because it allows you to finally learn exactly what your intuition is and where to find it, and you start relying on it, heavily.

See, before inner work, many of us confuse *intuition* with *paranoia* and operate from the place of paranoia because our first instinct is to second guess ourselves; this is because before inner work, a lot of us were surrounded by others who hadn't done their inner work either, thus forever second guessed themselves, and without any realization, encourage us to do the same. I now know and understand how important it is to have and maintain a strong sense of self, because when you don't, well… *majority will fucking rule you.*

But when we start doing our inner work? Oh, man. Slowly but surly that paranoia dissolves, freeing our intuition from underneath it. Then, once our intuition is free, we can finally hear *ourselves* instead of the noise that came from everyone else, and once we can hear ourselves, we can start *trusting ourselves*. We no longer need sixty red flags to pile up in front of our eyes before we acknowledge that something isn't right. Nah. The moment something doesn't *feel* right, we trust *that feeling* and move accordingly. Our intuition becomes all the proof we need.

So, we're doing *allllll* of this work and feel ourselves getting better and better at life! And because we're getting better at life, naturally, we start to change, and as a result, so do our interests, our conversations, the way we communicate, the people we want to be around, etc. Our tolerance levels for bullshit stops existing. We're not interested in being around people who only want to gossip all day. We're not interested in being around people who only want to complain all day. We're definitely not interested in being around people who are *always fucking negative*—which is not to be confused with those having *moments* of negativity—there is a huge difference between the two. We're not interest in being around people who refuse to ever take accountability. We're not interested in being around people who refuse to do any of *their* work, but instead want to reap the benefits of the work we've done and are continuing to do for ourselves… and suck us fucking dry. Why? Because once we are feeding ourselves with the good shit, *we understand that we need to protect ourselves*.

It's as if we become these growing fruit trees—and we all know that fruit trees need a very specific climate which includes lots of sunlight in order to grow.

But then we look around and realize that not too many other people are growing with us. Why? Because the majority of people, well… would rather stay with the majority of people. Here's the thing:
I used to say the phrase, "misery loves company", like I'm sure we all have, and I've always understood it's meaning; but prior to me beginning to do my inner work, I only understood it for what it meant on the surface.

A few years into my inner work and "misery loves company" is way deeper than what I had thought.
Misery is just a surface word for *toxicity*.
Misery is just a surface word for *hyper-negativity*.
Misery is just a surface word for abusive behaviour.
Misery is just a surface word fucking *hell*.

So, when I looked up and realized that I was alone in this growing stuff, for the most part, I understood the reason…

So many people are afraid of being alone with themselves, and more than that, cringe at the thought of doing work that is hard, and so… why would the majority spend so much time *alone, working hard* to create a peaceful, happy, *healthy* environment for themselves when they have so much more company, and so little work to do in fucking hell?

Which brings me back to what Bria was talking about—I *talk.*
When men get around me, if something ain't right, I address it head on. I call shit out! Not aggressively, but assertively.
Listen, as someone who never spoke up for myself, I didn't work this hard to unblock my throat chakra just to shut up all over again—no, ma'am.

If I'm dating a man and he oversteps a boundary of mine, **I voice it**, "Hey, you did ______, and it didn't sit will with me because ______. Please don't do that again."
If a man I'm dating decides to talk *at* me instead of *to* me, **I say**, "Whoa... don't do that. I don't speak to you in that way, don't do it to me."
If a man I'm dating begins to display an air of, "I have a penis, therefore I am above you, woman", **I'm calling for a full fucking**

pause, "*Heeey*.. I'm not your subordinate so I won't tolerate that type of energy, therefore, kindly do what *you* need to do to fix it."
If I'm dating a man and I know that I am meeting all of *his* needs, yet I find *my* needs being neglected, oh… **he's going to hear about that!** "*Heeeeeeeeey*... my needs are important too, and if for whatever reason under the golden sun you're not able to meet them, just let me know so that we can go our separate ways with no hard feelings."

You would think this is simple shit, right? Well, *appareeeeently* it fucking isn't.
My speaking up has sent many men either, A – Into a raging fit, complete with gaslighting and deflection, which… *K, buddy... whoa?* Or B – Quietly high-tailing in the opposite direction. And I'm not going to lie… both scenarios have hurt equally.

For one, too many times I've been left feeling like, *"Okay, soooo, should I just start dumbing myself down? Go back to shutting up and suppressing my own needs? Am I supposed to be lowering myself JUST to keep a man? Just to make a man feel better himself? Just to make a man feel more comfortable around me?"*

And for two, it's made me think of just how many women out there are doing those exact things—throwing away all of the hard work they had begun doing within, and lowering themselves, simply because they feel like it's better to do that and keep a man, rather than have no man at all and wait for the right one to show up for them. Patience is a virtue, and there is no better example of that than staying *alone* while you *wait* for the *right man*, instead of lowering yourself just to be able to say you have someone.

I, for one, refuse to throw away all of my hard work. Yes, I had a moment of frustration, and still have them from time to time because I'm ready to start building a life with a proper partner. I'm ready to share together, grow together, have a child together, laugh together, cry together, face challenges together, get over obstacles together and build bridges together.
Most of my twenties was the chapter where I was ready, willing and wanting to hold someone's hand. But this chapter?
Chapter 34 is the one where I will only extend my hand to someone who is ready, willing and wanting to hold my hand, too.

Some of these men just want a woman who will shut up and be grateful for the crumbs being lazily thrown on the ground for her to gobble up. Well, in chapter 34, I ain't no bird; I'm a whole fucking fruit tree, and a fruit tree I shall remain, sir.

The next day, Bria and I revisited our conversation, and the words she left me with are the words I'm going to leave you with:

"B, whatever you do, *do not settle*. You are way too much of a woman to be with any man who isn't going to be proud of you, cherish you, and love the entire shit out of you for exactly that—*all of the woman you are*."

Remix

"You attract what you are."

Like many of us, I grew up believing in that saying because I heard it so much; and to a certain extent, I still believe in it depending on the situation because context is literally everything. For example: When I was broken, I flocked to broken men just as much as broken men flocked to me, and it made sense because, well, shit… *I was broken.* I don't know too many whole men who are like, "Where are all the broken women who don't love themselves enough yet and let people walk all over them? Man, can't wait to find one, marry her and start a family with her!"—yeah, no.

In the context I'm going to elaborate on, however, "You attract what you are" just ain't the fuck it.

As I began getting very deep into my inner work and rising to meet higher versions of myself, I realized that I was still attracting very fucking broken people (both men and women, alike), and there came a point when I thought I was going crazy. *"I know that I'm rising, I know that I'm doing better, I know that I am not radiating broken energy anymore... so what the fuck, fam?"*

I needed answers, so I began asking questions, which lead me down a path of intensive research. Now, I'm a spiritual person (which is not to be confused with religious), and have a relationship with both God and the Universe as I believe they are two separate higher powers. That said, whenever I have questions about *myself* I do two things: 1- I pray and ask God to give me patience, strength and guidance. 2 – I wrap my questions into my energy, then give that energy to the Universe because the Universe is quite literally our sounding boards and whatever energy we give it, it gives back to us in return. Therefore, if I wrap my questions into my energy, the Universe will open up for me when the time is right, and provide a means for me to gain clarity. This means can be anything from a quote I stumble upon on Instagram that has something to do with my questions, and leads me to a whole book that I never knew existed, to an actual person coming to me and speaking about the very things I had been questioning.

With this round of questions, my answer came to me about a week or so later through a woman named, Jane, who has been keeping up with my journey as an author since I began sharing bits and pieces of my work through Facebook notes back in 2008. She lives in the same city as I do, Montreal, and though till this very day we've never actually met in person, she has supported and rooted for not only my work, but for me as a woman, too, which… hello? How fucking dope is that? I'm grateful, man. So grateful. Anyway…

One night after ending a very heated Instagram Live session, Jane and I ended up exchanging DM's (something we had very rarely ever done before), and during that exchange she told me that I was a lightworker. Now, I had no idea what the fuck that meant as I had never heard that word before, and she said to me, "You are transitioning, and in order to know how to do this, you need to know yourself 2000%. Look it up. Even if you just look up something simple on IG like, **#Lightworker**, you'll find quotes that will hit you like a ton of bricks." I knew the minute she said that, it wasn't by coincidence. What I had ask for and wrapped my energy in had been delivered, and I did not need to hear the message twice in order to take it seriously.

I began researching right away, and the first thing I needed to know was what the fuck a **Lightworker** even was:
In a nutshell, lightworkers are those who possess incredibly old souls that shine brightly through them and are here to help others heal, and each lightworker has their own unique way of doing so; however, while most have always been aware of their want to help heal others on some level or another, they have no idea of their truest or *highest* purpose, nor of the light that shines through them which is what attracts the broken, the lost, the confused—anyone who feels they are in the dark—until they go through some sort of awakening, which is often a spiritual one.

Jane was right, merely finding out what a lightworker was hit me like a ton of bricks, but also settled with my spirit, immediately. Everything made sense and I hadn't even got past the actual definition yet, but then, in an instant, a feeling of intense shyness crept up to wash away my feeling of relief.
Me? A lightworker? Come on, fam.
So… I'm just supposed to walk around like, "Yep, I have a light and people gravitate to me because of iiiiiittttttt!"? That's hella arrogant, no.

Self-sabotage at it's finest.

The moment I heard the words leave my mouth I scolded myself for having allowed them to ever enter my brain and interrupt this moment of clarity for me.

Being a humble human being is amazing, but a lot of us humble folks have allowed society to condition us into believing that being humble means to never claim our gifts from God and the Universe out loud, or any positive things about ourselves for that matter, because if we do, then we're arrogant and think we're better than everyone else.
Society vibrates low as fuck sometimes.
Again, *misery fucking loves company.*
If this is not a perfect example of why inner work is not a one-stop shop, but a journey for the rest of your life, I don't know what is. Even with all the work I had already done, I still had a moment of regression that I had to pull myself out of, and quickly, before it had time to spiral into a tornado of other negative shit, potentially causing me to rebuke my own damn gift. Whew, Chile!

With every higher level you unlock in your life, there will always be a new devil waiting to meet you there to tear you back the fuck down. Sometimes that devil shows up as a person, sometimes it shows up as a thought (self-sabotage), but no matter how it shows up, you have to be ready to kick its ass; and that day, your sis kicked some ass and claimed what had always been mine to begin with.

I am a problem solver, a mediator, a good listener, a secret-keeper, a nurturer, a motivator; and while I, myself, was once broken as fuck, I inspire others by being determined to figure shit out as I go along and not giving up on myself—all of that is what makes up my light. So, yes, like moths to a flame, different types of broken people gravitate towards my light for different reasons:

Some just need my light for a small moment to help them find their own light within themselves.

Some have no intention of finding their own light, and just want to leech off mine for as long as I will allow them.

Then there are some who straight up cannot stand the fact that I have a light that shines so brightly, and only goal is to put it out by any means necessary.

Claiming my light meant really understanding how important my energy was, why it needed to be protected at all costs, and which people and situations deserved it; which meant I needed to learn how to *discern* between the different types of broken people who came around me, and move accordingly.

Me being a light doesn't mean I'm some angelical figure who floats through life in a white dress with magic wand. Like, what the…? No.
Me being a light also doesn't mean that I have an abundance of emotional and mental space to take on everyone else's problems—no! I am human as fuck, and like everyone else, I struggle with my own fair share of shit that I have to sort out/find a way to fix.
Me being a light doesn't mean that I walk around all day screaming, "I DON'T KNOW WHO NEEDS TO HEAR THIS, BUT… I'M A LIGHT, SO… YEAH."
No.

Being a light doesn't mean that I have all of the answers, **because I really don't and never will**, but rather, when I've learned something from someone or have figured something out on my own, I simply share it for someone else who may need it so that that they can use it for their own journeys.

I have been writing since I was a little girl, and while I could have been writing about anything, unbeknownst to me, there was a reason why I always ended up writing about the things happening in my own life and turning them into stories in my little diaries.

"Lightworkers are those who possess incredibly old souls that shine brightly through them and are here to help others heal, and each lightworker has their own unique way of doing so..." — writing stories about the things I've been through and lessons I've learned, then sharing them with the world is *my* unique way of working my light, and now I'm able to see that God and the Universe had been preparing for my purpose (working my light) my entire life.

It's important to always remember that we all have our own purpose here, some of us recognize ours later than others and vice versa, but everyone has *their own* path and journey to take to do so. *My* self-love/inner work journey sent me down a path of spirituality, which led me to a spiritual awakening, which led me to a closer relationship with God and the Universe, which led me to leaning on and trusting in both to work *with* me, *through* me and others (like my big sis, Jane), which led me to a clear understanding that **sometimes we don't attract what we are, but instead, we attract what needs us.**

Get vex money

When my friends and I were growing up, before we left the house to go *anywhere* our parents/aunties/elders would ask, "You have get vex money on you?" Basically what that meant was, "Do you have enough money to find your own way home in case something pops off, you want to leave but your friends don't, you miss the last bus/metro and need to grab a cab, etc."
As a rule of thumb, if you didn't have it, then you had *no business* going a gawt damn place because *anything could happen out there.* Get Vex Money became something that many of us took with us into our adulthood. Example:

It's all well and good that a man who has money wants to "take care" of you. LOVELY. But *don't* just kick back and *depend* on that shit because **that's not smart.** Always make sure you have your own income coming in, be it big or small, and stack that so if shit ever hits the fan you're not completely assed out. Feel me?

Great that your homegirl is the one driving y'all to the club that night; but what if when it's time to leave, for whatever reason, she can't drive y'all back?

Great that homeboy is picking you up for a date, like a gentleman; but what if halfway through the date he turns out to be an asshole and you need to get the fuck out of there ASAP?

Moral of the story?

Always have your **Get Vex Money**, sis.

Big Sis Talks x 4

Jazzy, Angel, Erika and I were at Nathan's house, sitting around the table with a few of his boys, playing Dominoes. Well, Erika and I were playing with a couple of his boys while Jazzy and Angel sat alongside of us. Nathan, a guy I was seeing, was having a small house party/chill night, and Dominoes were Erika and I's shit, so naturally when the games started, we called next!

"Oh, B ain't no joke at this table," Nathan said to his boys as he brought me a glass of Pinot and kissed my forehead.
"You just sayin' that 'cause she's yo girl and you have to, otherwise, she gon' put the paws on ya," one of them joked.
Nathan laughed, "Naahh, I'm tellin' y'all for real. She ain't got no type of chill at this table, so don't say y'all haven't been warned." I lifted my chin all the way up and gave his boys a, "What my baby said" look, and my girls fell out laughing.
"Well, damn," Angel blurted, "Can I get a man to bring me a drank too? *Shiiiieeet.*"
On cue, Nathan's younger brother, Devron, stepped in beaming from ear to ear, "Allow me," he cooed.

"Boy!" Angel snapped, and we all busted out laughing again. Devron had just turned eighteen and had the hugest crush on Angel—it was hilarious. Every time we came around to any family friendly event that Nathan was having, and Devron was there, he spent his whole time trying to shoot his shot with Angel.

"What?" Devron asked, grinning, "C'mon, Angel, you ain't even that much older than me!"

"Yeah, Angel," Erika said, slamming a domino on the table while smirking, "What's ten years, some after school homework and a few handwritten notes to his math teacher explaining why he was late?"

"I'm gonna kick yo ass," Angel shot at Erika, "Nathan, come get your brother, please, dang!"

By this time, we were all laughing so hard that even Angel couldn't help but join in to laugh at herself.

"I'll grab you a drink," Nathan said, still laughing, and Angel popped her neck, "Thank you."

"I love that he's such a gentleman," Jazzy approved, and I beamed. "He truly is. Nathan's the best."

"I take after my brother, you know," Devron flirted, looking over at Angel.
"Good!" she exclaimed, "Being a gentleman nowadays is damn near a lost art. So keep being one while courting girls *your own age*."
"Devron, leave Angel alone nuh man," I fake scolded with a smile.
One of Nathan's boys, who also had a crush on Angel, looked over at her, "Aiight, so now I know you like a man who is a gentleman and will court you. Bet. What else do you like? What's your type?" Jazzy, Erika and I exchanged glances as we kept ourselves from laughing out loud at the thought we all knew we were thinking—*not you!*

Nathan came back into the room with a glass of Pinot for Angel and handed it to her.
"Thank you, Nathan," she said, then crossed her legs, took a sip, pursed her lips and batted her eyelashes at his boy, "If you must know, I like a man who is respectful, has a sense of humour and can laugh at himself, is loyal, and treats women like the queens we are..."

"Amen!" Jazzy and Erika declared.
"Mhhmmhhmm, girl. You betta say that

shit!" I added, slamming a domino on the table.

"I like a man who takes initiative, but also respects the boss in me. Knows when take charge *and* when to fall the fuck back 'cause I got it," she continued, and we acted like her hype-men in the background, adding *yep's* and *hello's* in between.

"He's gotta be *fiiinne*, you know, like myself—match my fly and shit. A little rough around the edges, but not too rough that he don't know how to muhfuckin' act. I like a man who is caring, compassionate, and can speak to my mind, body and soul with his actions, not just his words. Oh, and speaking of my body…" she licked her lips, seductively, as she kept her eyes fixed on Nathan's boy, "I like a man who knows how to work every angle of it with *hunger* and *passion*. Kisses *aaallll* the way down it, as wet as between my legs, then a swift, steady and patient tongue to work the most precious part until I… release. Then, slow, *deep* strokes while he's inside of me to bring me there again. I like a man whose goal is to make sure I get mine, a couple of times, before he gets his. A, *ladies first* mentality… if you will."

Angel had made sure to perfectly enunciate every word that she purred while keeping her eyes locked on Nathan's boy, and it was taking everything in Jazzy, Erika and I not to literally fall over with laughter and ruin her show. We knew her well enough to know exactly what she was doing.

While she was indeed telling the truth about her type of man, she knew damn good and well that Nathan's boy wasn't close to even *half* of those things. The joke was, Angel got a real-life high off of getting men like him all worked up, *hypnotized*, then suddenly knocking them out of their trance with a bold, rude awakening. I sat there wishing I could have filmed the look on Ol boy's face. All that was missing was drool coming down the side of his lip—shit was priceless.

Angel caressed the side of her thigh as she continued and I looked over at Devron, whose eyes were glued to her curves, probably silently begging god to let her give him just one night to prove he's up for the task(s). Then I took a peek at the rest of the men in the room, and sure enough, they were all hanging on her every word. Lawd! *Men are so easy, yo. Pussy really does run the world.*

Nathan, who was standing behind me, gently swept my hair to the side of my shoulder, bent down and placed a soft kiss on the back

of my neck then whispered in my ear, "She's lowballing herself with that couple of times, talk. Real men make sure their ladies are *completely* spent before they…" He purposely didn't finish his sentence knowing that my mind would flood with visions of our love making. I shivered with delight, then bent my head all the way backwards so he could kiss my lips, and he did so without missing a beat. I suddenly couldn't wait for the night to be over and for everyone to leave so that he and I could have our own… *after party*.
Nathan massaged my shoulders as we turned our attention back to The Angel Show and her audience, just in time her grand finale—the bold, rude awakening.

"And… last but not least," she smiled, slyly, then quickly changed her tone from seductive to matter of fact, and smacked her lips together, "I like a man with *proper money*. Paper. Bank rolls. Gwap. Dinero. *Benjaaamiiinnnsss*." She held up her free hand in Ol' boys face, rubbed her fingers together, dramatically, then snapped them three times in a zig-zag motion. If there was anyone in the room who didn't already know what type of man he *wasn't,* they sure as shit found out in that moment as the change of the expression on his face told it

all before he could open his mouth to tell on himself. His face went from looking like he was on the brink of an orgasm, to looking like someone threw a glass of cold water in it, and no one in the room could help but to fall the fuck out.
Jazzy high-fived Angel while a couple of the dudes around the table shook their heads as they gathered themselves.

Embarrassment danced inside of Ol' boy eyes, and he nodded, "*Oooohhh*, so you's a gold-digger type of chick. It's all good, ma. Now I know *you* ain't *my* type. Saved me a round of courting." Oh, baby boy was big triggered and his bag of feelings!
Angel fixed her lips for a clapback, but I gave her a look that said, "let me take this". She smiled at me, then eased her back against her chair and took a sip of her drink. The floor was mine, and it was clapback with a lesson time—my area of expertise.

"Uh, excuse me? Let me put you onto something real quick," I began, my tone dripping with attitude as I glared at him. "Welp, here she comes!" Nathan called out, and I continued, "A woman who sustains herself financially and wants a man who can also sustain himself financially is not a gold-digger, baby boy. She's an adult who is

interested in a partnership—not a subscription to the fucking babysitters club. Grow up."
"I know that's right!" Erika hollered.
"Get him, B!" egged on, Jazzy.
"Ah *shiiieet*, son. She served you!" Devron shouted with his fist over his mouth, and all the rest of the guys began crackin' on Ol' boy. "*You wasn't reeeaaaddyy*," one cried. "Son, she said the babysitters club," another managed through a laugh.

"Nah, hold up, hold up!" O'l boy protested. "See, that's the problem with a lot of you chicks. Look how she emphasized the money part," he moved his eyes from me back over to Angel, "Money isn't everything, ma, and that's why a lot of y'all are out single as fuck. Y'all keep passing up on good men all 'cause their pockets aren't fat!"

"First of all," Jazzy interjected, flipping her hair. "Who is *y'all*?"
"Abort mission!" one of the guys yelled.
"Back away, slowly. I repeat! *Back. Away. Slowly*," another grinned.
"Okay, maybe not *y'aaalll*," he motioned towards all of us women who were in the room, then continued, "But generally

speaking, this is why a lot of chicks are single."

I rolled my eyes at his deflection speech. "Awww," Angel sang, "On a level from one to *big mad*, exactly how *big mad* would you say you are right now?" More laughter rang out and Ol' boy shook his head, "I ain't mad."

"Yes you are! *You ain't gots to lie, Craig*," I teased. "Everything was sweet until Angel mentioned a man having money, then all of a sudden, shit got real bitter for you, real quick, and here you are trying to flip the script talkin' 'bout gold diggers and women being single 'cause they want men with money. Know what? Here, I'll throw you a bone. Money isn't everything— *agreed!* But it sure as hell pays the rent or mortgage, light bill, the groceries, the phone bill, the internet bill, the Netflix bill, the car note, the gas for the car, the dinners, the outings, the vacations… need I go on? We happen to live in a society where, even if you want to live with the minimal necessities—roof over your head, food in your fridge, heat in your house and clothes on your back—you still need some money, honey. SO, if you think for five seconds that a woman who *works* for *her* money should be linking up with, or even slightly entertaining a man who doesn't have a pot of his own to piss in all in the name of *money isn't everything*, or calling her a *gold-digger* because men without *money of their own* aren't her type?..." I let out a dramatic laugh then proceeded, "YIKES. But hey, to each their own so, go off, Beloved. Go the fuck off."

Angel reached across the table and we high-fived each other, while Erika called out, "And that, my friends, is a little something our crew likes to call…"
"CLAPBACKS WITH A LESSON!" all four of us sang together.

Ol' boy looked over at Nathan, and Nathan shrugged his shoulders, "I told y'all that she wasn't no joke at this table. Y'all thought I was only talkin' about Dominoes, though." Ol' boy shook his head but couldn't help but to crack a grin, "Aiight, aiight, yo. When you put it that way, it makes sense. All y'all are right, okay? On tonight's episode of Battle of the Sexes, y'all won this round!"

"It isn't even about winning a round more than it is about pointing out how dumb y'all sound sometimes," Jazzy said. "We women are out here pulling our own weight and working hard to secure our own bags so that

we *don't* have to depend on no man, and the fact that we get called gold diggers for expecting any man who wants to be with us to pull *his own weight* and have *his own* bags secured, too, is fucking absurd and exhausting."
"That part," I hummed, pointing my finger toward Jazzy.

Devron walked over to me and held his fist out for a daps, "Real talk, this is why I love you for my brother. Not only 'cause he's a whole happy ass nigga since you've been around, but 'cause you're smart and you surround yourself with other smart women. Every time you come around, whether by yourself or with your squad, I know I'm gonna learn some shit. You're like the big sis, all of y'all are, well… except Angel 'cause she's wifey." He grinned wide at Angel and she shook her head but smiled at him, nonetheless. Hella flattered by his words, I too smiled and gave him his daps, "And you're the little bro! I gotchu young buck. *We* gotchu." Nathan gave him a brotherly pat on the back then looked over and winked at me, and I blushed.

"Angel," Ol' boy began, and she eyed him. "Yo, my bad for calling you a gold-digger and shit. In my defence, there are a lot of

gold-diggers out here! But, you clearly ain't one of them, so… my bad." Jazzy, Erika and I applauded and Ol' boy rolled his eyes.
"Yo, don't be rolling yo eyes and shit!" Erika scolded. "We may check niggas when we need to, but we also give credit where credit is due. Nuff people, especially dudes, don't know how to apologize for shit, so take this applause my G. Gawt damn."
He chuckled then put up his hands signaling his surrender, "Aiight, aiight. Facts! I'll take it." He turned his attention back to Angel, rubbed his hands together and licked his lips LL Cool J style, "*Soooo*, now that we've made up, what do you sa…"
"Full stop," Angel ordered, cutting him off mid-sentence, "You still ain't *my* type, homie."

Laughter erupted once more throughout the room as Ol' boy humbly took his L with a shoulder shrug and a smile, and we changed the topic.

You see, we women ain't the only ones who can benefit from a good ol' fashioned Big Sis Talk.

So, you don't have a boyfriend?

And? Girl! Do you know how many amazing things you can be accomplishing during this time? Do you?

Go live your life! Key word being, *your*.

Go get yourself two-three new hustles and stack some money. Go take those road-trips with your homegirls. Go on some dates just for fun. Go write that book you've always wanted to write. Go finish that course you never got around to finishing because you were too busy crying over some human with testicles who wasn't even a good human, period. Like, hello?

So you don't have a boyfriend… *awesome*.

Go enjoy your single life, boo!

Fucking, yes

I like seeing women stand up for themselves, catching themselves three seconds before they're about to walk back into some shit that they've worked so hard to walk away from and be like, "Actually, no. Fuck this, and fuck you."

That, for me, is inspiring.

Block and Delete

"I miss you," I began to write in the text message. "I miss the man you used to be for me. The one who used to make me blush, constantly, and caress my soul ever so gently. I miss the warm light that used to dance in your eyes as you'd stare at me, causing butterflies to flutter throughout my tummy, magically. I miss the way you used to speak to me. All of the endearing little nicknames you had for me. It sounds small, trivial even, but I'm a simple woman and it's the little things that mean the most to me. I miss filling the pages of my notebook with the story of a romance that blossomed between two people, suddenly and organically. Instead, the story I pen now is one of a man I gave my heart to who changed drastically…"

I sat, read the text message back to myself and took a sip of my wine. "Never mind," I whispered, and deleted the whole thing.

It had been weeks since he and I had spoken, and I began scrolling through our message box reading our last few conversations. Arguing, name calling, more arguing, more name calling. I took another sip of my wine and shook my head, "What was I thinking? About to throw my ass right back into the fire," I chuckled. "Nah, B. It's *over*, over." Then I delete the entire message box, blocked his number and deleted it out my phone.

Welcome to Triggerville

"So, when are you gonna have some kids, girl?" Ashely asked me.
I've always hated whenever people asked me that question. I understand that most people who already have kids ask it as a way to make conversation, and don't mean any harm, but damn… what ever happened to the, "So, about this weather?" smalltalk starter-kit?

I was at a birthday dinner for a girl I used to work with prior to becoming a full-time author. She wasn't my *homegirl*, homegirl, but we had always been pretty close as co-workers; so when she invited me to her birthday dinner, I was down to attend. I didn't really know too many other people seated at the table, with the exception of Ashely and her two rollies, Jessica and Carla—a trio of besties whom I was familiar with because we had all lived in the same area of the city back in the day, and it just so happened that they were friends of the birthday girl.
I had moved away from that end of the city a long time ago, so it was very rare that we ever bumped into one another out and about, and on the extremely odd occasions that we

did, it was a quick, "Oh, hey, girl!" and we kept it moving. There wasn't any beef or anything of that nature, we just weren't friends like that. Know what I mean?
We were, however, all friends on Facebook, so most of what we knew of each other came directly from our own mouths via status updates.

All three of them began having kids during their late teens and early twenties, and ever since Facebook existed, all three of them had used status updates as their personal diary entrees, thus making everyone privy to all of their personal business—including the never-ending sagas with their baby's daddy's. Who needs soap operas or reality TV when you have Facebook? Am I right or am I right?

Ashely, Jessica and Carla were notorious for spilling *aallll* of their own tea, then telling anyone who dared make a comment about such tea to mind their own business. I mean, I never really understood people like that, but hey, maybe those type of people were never meant for me to understand, anyway. Most of the tea throughout the years was hella repetitive. Facebook: "What's on your mind?"

Ashely: “My baby daddy’s ain’t shit. All three of them.”

Jessica: “This time, I’m really taking my baby daddy to court for child support. SORRY, NOT SORRY, but five hundred dollars a month is NOT ENOUGH!”

Carla: “My baby daddy over there playing house with another woman when he hasn’t seen his child in a month!”

Ashely: “LOL! One of my baby’s daddy’s got engaged. HA! Guess some chicks like taking trash off the streets.”

Jessica: “HAPPY FATHER’S DAY TO MUTHAFUCKIN’ MEEEEEEEEE.”

Carla: *Posts flyer of a party*
“Who wants to pay my ticket for this next week ‘cause yo girl is *broke*, broke!”

Ashely: “I need a sugar daddy ‘cause I’m tired of working for peanuts.”

Jessica: “Watching all these bitches taking trips out the country every few months, like, MUST BE NICE TO HAVE TRAVEL MONEY. Ugh.”

Yep… same shit on rinse and repeat since 2010 when we all added each other.

I moved my newly dyed blonde ringlets out of my face and smiled, "Oh, I'm not trying to do all that right now. Birth control, condoms and I are getting along just fine," I responded short but polite.

Now, I had been in this very space *many* times before. Something about being a woman without any children sitting at a dinner table with women who already have children makes you a target for this type of question… so I had learned.
I had also learned from past experiences that *my* honest, in depth reasons as to why *I* wasn't interested in having children yet tended to always *trigger* someone else, and I just wasn't trying to go there that evening. My hope was for Ashely to pick up on my shortness, shrug her shoulders and say something along the lines of, "I hear you, girl," then move on to another topic. But, nope. *Nooooooo*. What's having hope when you're around people who need to be all up in your uterus?

"Whatchu mean you *ain't tryna* do all that right now?" she pressed on, almost mockingly. "Yeah. What are you, like…

early thirties?" Carla snickered nodding her head toward me, "That clock is ticking, suga. Tick tock."
"Besides," Jessica decided to add, "You don't want to wait till you're forty to have kids, sis. Think about it. You'll be *fifty* by the time your kid is ten, you'll barely have any energy left and who wants to be an old ass mom to a young ass kid, anyway? Where's your man at? Tell him it's baby making time."

Okay, WOW! I thought to myself. Thank god my girl, Erika, wasn't with me because the way she would have flown across that table and laid SOLID hands on those three bitches… Whew! The levels of DISRESPECT were all the way through the fucking roof. Bruh!

What if I didn't have any kids yet because I kept having miscarriages? Matter of fact, what if I'd just had a miscarriage the week prior, and broke down into a waterfall of tears at the damn table thanks to them pressing me? What if I didn't have any kids yet because my body physically wouldn't allow me to due to a complication? Why would I have to explain my complication to anyone, let alone three chicks who weren't part of my life in any way, shape or form?

Or, here's a cool thought: what if *when* or *if* I was going to have kids was simply none of anyone's *muthafuuuuckin'* business? Oh, wait… it *wasn't* anyone's muthafuckin' business. Look at that!

You know, it's one thing to ask, "When are you going to have some kids?", and not mean any harm. It's a whole other thing when the woman you asked that question to responds but doesn't offer to volunteer any more personal information after the fact, and not only do you keep fucking pushing her, but you're disgustingly disrespectful on top of it!

Tell them to shove their highly inappropriate questions and disrespectful as fuck comments up their no etiquette havin', probably only going to order an appetizer 'cause they can't afford these meal prices, asses, a voice inside of me whispered through gritted teeth. And you know what? Normally I would have told them exactly that, however, I was smack in the middle of working on myself, and part of my self-work was learning how to control my reactive ass emotions and not to lower myself to meet other people at their low ass vibrational levels. PLUS, it was a birthday dinner, and the last thing I wanted to do was ruin it by causing a whole scene. I *loathed* being in the middle of any scene, period, let alone being the cause of one.

Whooosah, B. Whoos-the-fuck-aaaaah.

"That's cool," I smirked, keeping my rising body temperature, emotions and the tone of my voice in check. "I'll be that forty-year-old mom who's financially free and is her own boss—thanks to the business I'll have had time to put all of my energy and hard work into—and both my child and I can have the luxury of being able to afford everything we need *and* want. I'll have mastered loving myself deeply and unapologetically, which in turn, will allow me to be able to teach my child self-love by way of example rather than just talk. Talk is cheap without the actions to back it up.
Not to mention, mastering how to love myself will assist me greatly in choosing the right man *to* have a child with. One who is responsible, secure within himself, emotionally intelligent *and* available, respects and loves himself, is my homie first and loves me *properly*.
Again, being the example for my child is important to me, and I don't want to be preaching things like self-love and respect while I'm in some struggle love

situationship with their father, disrespecting myself right in his or her face—no ma'am.

Don't me wrong, I know that I can seek a man out for all of these qualities, find him and everything is peachy, but then somewhere down the line shit ends up going left. People change, grow apart and break up all the time, and I'm not naive to that possibility being my reality by *annnny* stretch of the imagination. However, I strongly feel like the least I can do on my end is to make sure that before I go into something so life changing, I do so responsibly; and for me, responsibly means doing my best to set up a healthy environment for all parties involved prior to bringing a child into this world who didn't ask to be born."

I ended my explanation with the very shoulder shrug I had been hoping to get from Ashely, earlier, and took a sip of my champagne. During my "speech", I hadn't even noticed that the entire table had tuned in. "Now that was sexy! Are you single? Because I'll marry you right now. Whoosh!" a homeboy of the birthday girl said, suddenly.
"Damn, girl. Didn't know we were at church tonight, but shit, pass the collection plate

ova here 'cause that has to be one of the most refreshing sermons I have been to in a while, chile, yes!" another homegirl of the birthday girl sang.

I felt my face starting to get a little warm, and I knew I was blushing. My intentions weren't to be the center of attention like that *at all*. I just wanted to give the three musketeers what they'd asked for—the truth.

Ashely, Jessica and Carla sat across from me, fuming. I had hit a nerve in all three of them and it might as well have been etched in red marker on their foreheads.
"So, hold on," Ashely scowled, "Whatchu tryna say?"

Here the fuck we go.

I looked at her, confused. What I wanted to say was, "Bitch, I didn't stutter. Are you slow? I SAID WHAT THE FUCK I SAID, NOW FUCK OFF." But you know, the whole working on myself thing was still in the front of my mind, so I kept it classy instead, "You asked me a question, and I answered that question, directly, without any breaks, pauses or stumbling in between. I said exactly what I said *without trying*, sis."

Whew, go me.

"Nah, I think what you were tryna say was that because our baby's daddies ain't around and we fall on some hard times as single moms, that we ain't good moms or some shit—and that's fucking low of you."

Jason, another friend of the birthday girl who was seated next to me raised an eyebrow, "Uhhh, pretty sure I heard the entire conversation, and I'm pretty sure that's not even close to what she said."

I took another sip of my champagne and shook my head.

"Girl don't do that," the birthday girl quipped from three seats away, checking Ashely.

"Nah, it's all good," I assured, looking from her then back to Ashely and her click, "Sis, I never said you and your homies were bad moms. You asked me a question that was inappropriate from the jump, then y'all went on to further press me with even more inappropriate statements, talkin' bout my age *and* my muthafuckin' clock as if y'all are gonna be the ones helping me to raise this child when and *if* I have one. As if *my* muthafuckin' uterus is running on *y'alls* clock!"

"B..." the birthday girl tried to interrupt because she knew where it was about to go.

I had been doing *really well* with keeping my composure. Shit, up until that moment, I hadn't even let one cuss word escape my lips. But sis wasn't getting it through her fucking skull, and there was only so much I was willing to take from her before reading her for filth in my mind became reading her for filth *out loud*. Those three pressing ass bitches sitting across that table were going to learn a thing or two about me, minding their own fucking uteruses, *and* themselves. "Nah!" I continued, "Lemme tell y'all something: whatever decisions y'all have made, men y'all chose to procreate with, financial situations y'all are in, and anything else y'all got or don't got going on in y'alls lives have absolutely nothing to do with me, and furthermore, I'm well within my right *not* to want *y'alls* life for *myself*. The fuck? Y'all sat across this table and took DIRECT shots at my age *and* uterus, and now that you've heard me explain that I WOULD LIKE TO BE STABLE IN AS MANY AREAS OF MY LIFE AS POSSIBLE BEFORE BRINGING A CHILD INTO THIS WORD, you wanna flip the script and say that I tried to call y'all bad moms? Go heat up a warm cup of milk, drink it, then take a fucking nap, sis."

"BITCH?!" Ashely shouted, standing up.
"Ah shit," Jason mumbled, as everyone else at the table began telling her to sit down. I rested my back against the chair and shook my head, "Girl, first of all, ain't nobody scared of you. Second of all, this could have all been avoided had you just left me the fuck alone. Don't throw rocks then try to hide your hands—that shit is wack. Third of all, if you wanna fight me behind the things I want and don't want for MYSELF, then fuck taking a nap… go get some *therapy* 'cause you've got some shit you need to come to terms with that, once again, have *noooootthhiiiinnng* to do with me."

By this time, the whole restaurant was looking at us and the birthday girl had gotten up and made her way over to Ashely, "Girl, what is wrong with you?"
"Fuck her," Ashely spat, starring at me with daggers in her eyes.
Carla got up and rubbed Ashely's arm, gingerly, "Come on, girl. Forget her. Matter fact let's just go. You wanna leave?"
Jessica stood as well, "Yeah, let's just go. She ain't worth it."
I couldn't help but laugh at Jessica's words. *Yes, sis, that's right. Y'all started with me, but I'm the one who ain't worth it. Whatever the fuck helps y'all sleep at night, man.*

Ashely, who never took her eyes off of me, nodded, "Yeah, let's be out. Just the thought of that bitches old ass eggs rotting her stomach made me lose my appetite, anyway."

"Okay, NAH, now you really NEED to go," the birthday girl ordered.

"Food and drinks occupy my stomach, sis. My eggs get made in my ovaries, then find their way to my fallopian tubes... but continue to go off though." I winked at her and a few other women at the table giggled. Both Jessica and Carla shot me looks of death as Ashely swung her purse around her shoulder, "Fuck this hoe, she ain't shit. Let's be out before I beat her ass."

"Girl, goodbye!" one of the women at the table yelled, fed up. "You wanna beat someone's ass because they told the truth about themselves and your insecure ass feels some type of way 'cause it was the opposite of your truth—your truth that you clearly hate? Hurry up and leave, already. Try growing up on your way out the door, too. Foolishness."

"*Byyyyyeeeee!*" a few other people at the table called out in unison before the trio could say anything else.

"Is everything alright over here?" a concerned waitress stopped to ask.
"Yes, everything is fine," the birthday girl responded forcing a fake ass smile. "These three were just on their way out."

Ashely, Jessica and Carla made their way out of the restaurant while the rest of us watched. When they were gone, sis who had yelled, "Girl, goodbye!" turned to me, "You did good," she said. "I would have served them every name in the book the moment they started throwing shade on your age. I have a child, and my situation is neck and neck with theirs, especially Ashely's.
My baby daddy ain't shit, but if we're being honest, he wasn't shit before I got pregnant. I had no business being with his triflin' ass in the first place, but I was desperate. I was young, dumb and so damn desperate for any piece of a man that I stayed with him and took whatever bullshit attention he gave to me, which wasn't much might I add.
It was just dick. Dick that I got when *he* wanted to drop by. Dick that I got when *he* was horny for me. Dick that I got when *he* wanted to buss a nut. But again, I was so desperate, and all the sweet shit he would whisper in my ear while he was deep in my pussy, I believed.

He only used to tell me that he loved me while we were having sex. *Now* I know he wasn't talking to me, but to my pussy instead; but back then? Shit... I held onto those words. I *lived* by those words. I let him fuck my brains out, unprotected, and nut in me as much as he wanted. When I found out I was pregnant, I wasn't anywhere near ready for a child, but my exact thoughts were: *If I have this baby, then he'll stop all his games and want to be a family.*
The night I was in the hospital giving birth, he was at a hotel party in a jacuzzi with two other chicks in it, both all over him. The plot twist? One of the chicks was Ashely."

My mouth dropped to the floor hearing that last part, and she nodded her head as if she'd told the story a thousand times before and had gotten the same reaction every time. *Damn, this city is so big, yet so fucking small!*

"Yep," she continued, "Our kids are a year apart, and unfortunately, only get to hang out together when their father is around because Ashely's ass is too bitter and immature to be cordial with me for the sake of them… which is why I added the "grow up" part in there when she was on her way out this evening. See, while you were simply telling your truth, you were holding up a mirror to both Ashely and I's reality. The difference between her and I though, is that I was proud of you. All of what you said is exactly how shit *should* be before having a child. Now, don't get me wrong, I love my daughter and wouldn't trade her for anything, but please believe that I wouldn't *ever* want her to follow in my footsteps. I wouldn't want *any* woman to follow in my footsteps for that matter. Chicks like Ashely need to heal, forgive themselves for not knowing better back then, forgive the men who wronged them and let all that shit go. All that hate they carry in their heart is what causes them to lash out at other women instead of being able to applaud other women for wanting better for themselves."

I nodded my head, "Well, shit. A plot twist indeed, girl! Are you a writer? 'Cause that's *definitely* something for a book."
She laughed, "Nah, I don't write. That's all you, Cici. B."
I looked at her, surprised, "How did you know I…"
"I follow you on Instagram," she replied with a smile. "You do? Lawd, gawd! And the plot thickens! Yo, I literally *never know* who be following my ass. This is wild. I'm genuinely shocked over here, but in a good

way!" We shared a laugh as the birthday girl came over, "*Yooooo*, homegirl was *trippin'* trippin!" she blurted.
"Big facts," I responded, "But my bad for eve…" she held up her hand, cutting me off, "Nah, girl. *None* of that was your fault and you had every right to defend yourself. Shoot, I'm surprised you didn't go off on her sooner and harder than that, knowing you!" *Girl, you and me fucking both.* I thought.
"Yeah, well… I'm trying this new thing where I don't let people bring me down with them into their misery where they need company."

"Well, you definitely Michelle Obama'd her by going high when she went low. I mean, you put your own smartass spin on it with lesson about where eggs comes from, but that's what makes you, you." The three of us started laughing and after the birthday girl finally caught her breath, she flagged down the waitress to order two more bottles of champagne for the table. I turned to sis I was talking to prior, "Thank you, by the way, for having my back, for this talk, and also... I'm proud of you too, girl. There are a lot of Ashely's out there, but not too many of you."

She smiled, graciously, "Well, you keep writing your truths. I'm pretty sure that it will inspire a lot of women not to turn into the Ashely's, and hell, maybe you'll inspire a few of the Ashely's to be fed up of being the Ashely's." I beamed and nodded once more, "Will do."

Miami, December 14th, 2018

I was on the phone with my mom, sitting on the boardwalk by the water. I had just been betrayed and disrespected the fuck out of by not one, but *two* people in my life, back to back, who I trusted and loved with my whole heart. One was a man, who I was undoubtedly in love with, the other, a female friend who I would have done anything for… who I *had done everything for.*

"I'm tired," I whispered into the phone.
I closed my eyes as the weight of the pain from the heartaches sat on top of my heart, crushing it… suffocating it.
Before I knew it, I was crying loud and hard, and the tears were flowing down my cheeks like a running faucet. This shit hurt, man. It hurt. "What's the point?" I managed in between sobs. "What's the fucking point?! I'm tired, mom. I am *tiiiired*. What's the point of being good to people when all they end up doing is stabbing you in your chest? What's the point of being honest with people when all they do is lie to you? What's the point of being understanding and patient with people when all they do is take advantage of that shit? What's the point of going out of your way for people that you

love, only for them to spit disrespect and ungratefulness in your face? I don't want this heart of mine anymore, mom. I DON'T FUCKING WANT IT."

"Hey! HEY!" My mother responded, sternly. "You're going to stop these types of talks right now. Do you hear me? I know you're hurting. I know it's hard. Trust me, baby girl, I have been where you are a thousand times before—I KNOW. But you *cannot* say shit like that. You're talking about people being ungrateful and disrespectful in one breath, and in the next, there you are being ungrateful and disrespecting YOUR gift in life. Are you fucking kidding me right now? Listen to me and listen to me well: There is a *reason* that you are able to love the way you do, be there for people the way that you are, forgive people the way you do, and have compassion for people the way that you do—it's because YOUR BIG HEART IS YOUR GIFT AND YOUR BLESSING, and I don't ever want to hear you shit on it like this again. Look at how many fucked up, *evil* people there are in the world, baby girl. The world *needs* good hearted people to balance that shit out. Come on, you know this stuff already!

Why do you think that you make it through every single fucking storm you've ever been in? Why do you think that even when you are down on your luck, it's never *ever* for long? It's because with your GOOD HEART comes BLESSINGS.
Do you think people who have fucked up hearts and do wicked things to others are able to sleep well at night and be at peace with themselves?" She paused for a moment, waiting for me to answer.
"No," I whispered, wiping my eyes.
"Of course they don't—they can't! They have these demons haunting their spirits. That's what you want for yourself? To exchange your good heart for what they have?" She paused again. "No," I repeated.

By that point, I was coming out of my shitty moment and back into my proper senses. My mother was right—I *did* know all of this stuff already. I sniffled then exhaled, "I love you so much, mommy."

"I love you too my sweet girl, and I don't like hearing you like this. I am so proud of you. You have come such a long way and have accomplished everything you ever said that you would. Look at you! You are an author with NINE books. You help women all over the world by being brave enough to

share your stories and tell the truth about what you've been through in your life. You are so loved! You are appreciated. For fuck's sake, you're in Miami for the *whole* winter. Right now you're sitting in shorts and T-shirt, while we're all back home in Montreal, bundled up, dreading the snow we have to shovel tomorrow morning. You're able to be there *because* of all of your hard work, your dedication, your will, your passion, and *your good ass heart*. This is your time! You've *earned* it. Don't let these people ruin it for you. More than that, don't let these people win by consuming their negativity, turning you into them.
They have shit they need to sort out in their hearts that have nothing to do with you, and everything to do with them. So let them be and wish them well. Yeah, it hurts you now because have to let go of people you deeply care about. But imagine how much it's going to hurt them down the line when they realize that they had a woman who truly cared about them… and *they lost her*."

Broken record

I've never met a man who didn't know exactly what he was doing when he was doing it, and yet, we women will come up with every excuse under the golden sun for men who continue to treat us poorly, even after we've already explained to them in detail why what they're doing is not okay.

"He had a few bad weeks at work."
"He's under a lot of pressure right now because of his debt."
"He lost his job."
"He gets really bad migraines."
"The kids have been stressing him out."
"He spilled his coffee on himself and it was very hot."
"He's a Cancer, and is very sensitive to full moons and mercury retrogrades."
"His plant died, and he really loved that plant."

Bruh.

What the actual living fuck does *any* of that have to do with you?

As a rule of thumb that I've learned to adhere to, dear sista, always ask yourself:

1– Do you treat the man you love like shit?
2– Do you take all of the shit that you're going through that has nothing to do with him or your relationship *at all*, out on him?

If the answers are no, then what the fuck are you doing? **Someone who claims to love you doesn't treat you like shit**—and I know this, along with **doing your inner work** has been a repetitive theme throughout this entire book, but it's been repetitive on purpose because hopefully the more you read it written in different ways, by the end of this book it will stick.

These men aren't children out here; they are fully capable of understanding the difference between right and wrong. We should not have to repeat, "Hey, OUCH, YOU'RE HURTING ME," 2882839302 times to a person who claims to love us, nor should we have to handout excuses to all of our friends and family as to why that persons behaviour is downright deplorable as if they were goody bags after a party. Like, what?

No. Full fucking stop. This is bullshit! And for all the, "…but we have children together, I can't just leave," folks, and for those who don't have children with the dickhead they're with yet… consider this:

Do you want your children watching the way their father treats their mother like shit, the way their mother tolerates that treatment, then taking that example with them into their teens and adulthood, believing ***that*** is what love is and repeating the same cycle in their relationships?

I don't fucking think so.

• Read books that remind you of why you need to get out of the situation you're in with these types of men.

• Read books that speak to the importance of self-love and why you need it.

• Read books by female authors who aren't afraid of being honest about their experiences, and are straight forward with their cautionary tales.

• Read books that explain how the minds of these specific men work, and why ***you*** alone ***cannot*** and ***will not*** change them. (A good one is, Why Does He Do That by, Lundy Bancroft).

• Follow women who share words of encouragement and drop gems on Instagram.

•Listen to podcasts by women who make it their business to speak up about toxic relationships, the importance of emotional and mental health, etc.

• Get therapy.

• Find support groups online, offline in your area, or both.

Whatever you need to do to help you realize that the person inflicting pain on you, in any degree, **doesn't love you**, so you can move on and create a healthy environment for yourself, children and future children (if you want any)—**do it all.**

Roll call

Let this be the year that we, as women, practice making better choices for ourselves.

The year that we take all steps necessary in order to start focusing on what we're doing, what we're tolerating, what we're prioritizing and what we're ignoring.

If we know that we're good women, then why are we tolerating bad men in our lives, in our beds and inside of us?
If we know that we have a lot to offer, then why are we prioritizing men who ain't got shit to give back?
If we know what a damn red flag looks like, then why do we keep ignoring every one that pops up? Uh, uh. No more.

Y'all ain't tired? We're grown…

It's time to start making better choices for ourselves.

January 1st, 2019, I Affirmed

- New levels in my career.
- A tighter circle filled with real love, laughter, encouragement and genuine support.
- Unwavering trust in my energies and the energies of others.
- Unwavering trust in my purpose.
- More trips to different countries—be it with friends, a partner, or by myself.
- The fiercest, most confident version of myself that I have ever fucking been.

Reminder

Being in a happy, loving relationship with a man is dope. But, sis… your world cannot revolve around that man alone. *You need to **have** and **maintain** your own **identity.***

You can be cool with his friends and family, but don't isolate yourself from your own friends and family.

Definitely support his dreams and goals, but don't neglect your own dreams and goals. Meet his wants and needs, absolutely! (Within reason, obviously. Calm down), but make sure that your reasonable needs and wants are met as well.

Love the fuck out of him all day, yes! But don't you dare forget to love the fuck out of yourself first.

Being in a relationship with a man doesn't mean tossing the relationship you have with yourself out of the window, and I just feel like a lot of women need this reminder.

One last thing...

The Shovel

I've been the patient girl.
The tolerant girl.
The never speak up for myself girl.
The overly understanding girl.
The go out of my way for people girl.
The make excuses for people girl.
The put everyone I love before myself girl.

I've been the, "*It's fine*", when it really wasn't girl.
The, "*I'm just gonna let it slide*", girl.
The, "*Let me be the bigger person*", girl.
The, "*You're right, I'm wrong*", just to make peace girl.

I've been the, "*I need you*", girl.
The, "*Can't sleep without you*", girl.
The cry myself to sleep seven nights in a row girl.
The, "*Why don't you care*?", girl.
The, "*Why am I not enough for you*?", girl
The begging for a man to love me back girl.

And then… one day…

I became the **tired girl**.

There was a saying that I recalled,
"If you don't want to be someone's doormat,
then get up off of their floor."
And when I looked in the mirror,
I realized that I couldn't afford to be
what stared back at me, anymore.

I didn't see the woman
I wanted to be…
the woman who I knew was somewhere,
deep down, being suffocated inside of me.
Instead, I saw a welcome mat that read,
"Here… wipe your dirty fucking shoes all
over me."
And when I closed my eyes,
I saw a flash of all the people in my life
who were doing just that,
happily and unapologetically.

"Enough," I whispered to myself
as I felt the familiar sting of tears
beginning to form.
"ENOUGH!" I yelled at the top of my lungs,
as those tears began to rush down my cheeks
like a merciless rainstorm.
"I'm better than this," I managed through
my pain-filled cries.
"Aren't I better than this?" I asked god,
as the saltwater took over, blurring my sight.

I dropped to my knees,
and clasped my hands together
in front of me.
Then I let everything out,
every painful emotion that I was harbouring
inside of me.

"God, please," I began,
as my cold bathroom tiles
stuck to my bare skin.
"I can't be this girl anymore,
please help me.
Give me the strength to dig through
this mess I've made,
so I can uncover the woman who I know
lies within.
Lead me to the shovel
and I promise to do the work
that needs to be done.
I don't want to be this girl anymore, god…
she has overstayed her welcome."

After that day, I kept my promise
and made it a point to change my ways.
And I know you're probably reading this,
thinking, "Girl, what? It wasn't your fault.
No need to be so hard on yourself,
you were not the one to blame.
You were but a victim of other people's
piss poor behaviour.
It wasn't you. It was them.

They are the ones who needed to change."

But see, coupled with this context,
it's that very type of narrative
that doesn't help girls like the one
who stared back at me in my mirror
to progress.
The, "it's never you, it's always them"
mentality, doesn't serve as the food we need
to feed some of the most
important departments
that are starving inside of us—
accountability, responsibility, self-love,
self-respect and self-awareness.

Yes, the people who come into our lives
only to treat us like shit are foul, this is true.
But what is also true is that
we have a responsibility to ourselves,
and there has to come a point
when we admit that
what *we* allow… *will* continue.

There is this sense of entitlement
we tend to adhere to,
one that screams,
you owe me the love and respect
I give to you,
and it's one that I began to dismantle,
because actually…
no one owe us shit,

or has to do anything
that they truly don't want to do.

"We teach people how to treat us"
was a phrase I began repeating to myself
every morning, throughout the day,
and before I went to bed.
"IT IS my job to not only set the example,
but to walk away from anyone
who decides to disrespects this program."

You see, the woman I wanted to be,
the one I knew was deep down
inside of me…
She was full of life, free spirited,
and still had a heart that beat passionately,
but she was also assertive
and took no one's shit.
She stood and spoke up for herself
and did so, fearlessly.
The woman I wanted to be
knew her worth, loved herself,
and had some non-negotiable
muthafuckin' boundaries.

Today, when I look in the mirror,
I never feel tired of what I see.
Because gone is the girl
that was everyone's doormat,
and in her place is a woman
I am in love with,

one that I worked day and night
to unbury… and set free.

The moral of my story?
Forget all of the “them’s”
and focus on you.
If you are anything like the girl I *was*,
but want to start living *your* best life,
then you better boss up
and get your shovel my sis…

‘cause you’ve got some incredibly promising work to do.

BIG SIS TALKS

THE CRIMSON KISS QUOTE COLLECTION III

INSTAGRAM @THECRIMSONKISS

Previous books by Cici.B

Letters to My Ex

Blush

Lost and Found: The Book of Short Stories

Spilled Words: The Crimson Kiss Quote Collection

Girl Power: The Crimson Kiss Quote Collection II

12:02AM Volume1: Exploring B

The Little Book of Women's Pet Peeves

The Self-Love Bible: How I Learned to Love Myself

The Self-Love Bible Part 2: My 10 Dating Commandments

How I Built My Author Brand on Instagram: Inspiration, tips and tricks for authors and aspiring authors who want to do the same

BIG SIS TALKS

THE CRIMSON KISS QUOTE COLLECTION III

Made in the USA
Monee, IL
28 January 2021

58918246R00104